CRAVING GOD

60 DEVOTIONS FOR REAL WOMEN

LYSA TERKEURST

Also by Lysa TerKeurst

CRAVING GOD

60 DEVOTIONS FOR REAL WOMEN

LYSA TERKEURST

NEW YORK TIMES BESTSELLING AUTHOR

ZONDERVAN®

ZONDERVAN

Craving God: 60 Devotionals for Real Women
Copyright © 2013 by Lysa TerKeurst

Requests for information should be addressed to:

Zondervan, *Grand Rapids, Michigan 49530*

ISBN: 978-0-310-62036-5

Published in association with the literary agency of Fedd & Company, Inc., Post Office Box 341973, Austin, TX 78734.

Printed in the United States of America

13 14 15 16 17 18 /DCI/ 21 20 19 18 17 16 15 14 13 12 11 10 9 8 7 6 5 4 3 2 1

Contents

DAY 1

It's All in the Family

*The Spirit himself testifies with our spirit
that we are God's children.*

(ROMANS 8:16)

Thought for the Day: We are only one good choice away from being back on the path of perseverance. But no matter how far off the path or how long we have been on it, God is patient with us and loves us as a dearly beloved child — part of His family.

American humorist Erma Bombeck once said, "I come from a family where gravy is considered a beverage." Coming from the South, I can identify. Southern food culture taught me this: "If I love you, I will feed you — a lot!" And where did I often pile the most "love" on my plate? The church's covered-dish luncheons in the fellowship hall! Nowhere else could I get fried chicken, chicken-fried steak with sawmill gravy, sour cream mashed potatoes, with a side of spaghetti and meatballs. Then, of course, a "taste" of three different pies and some sweet tea to wash it all down. Boy, did it make the cooks happy to see my plate piled high! We called it "sharing the love."

So began my perception that food equals love. But like any unfaithful lover, food cannot love back. Overeating made me feel defeated and incapable. *Made to Crave* chronicles my one-sided love affair with food and the distress it caused me. That is, until my ever-expanding waistline and dismay caused me to direct my heart elsewhere.

As I began searching the Scriptures, I discovered how God can point our hearts to him: "May the Lord direct your hearts into God's love and Christ's perseverance" (2 Thessalonians 3:5). And I found some beautiful truths that help me to redirect my heart every day:

- *God's love never fails* (1 Corinthians 13:8). Even if we feel that we are weak and failing, God's love for us will never cease.

- *Nothing can separate us from God's love* (Romans 8:39). Not twenty, fifty, one-hundred, two-hundred pounds, or more — nothing will separate you from God's love.

- *Love is patient* (1 Corinthians 13:4). No matter how long we struggle to find victory in any area of our life, God is patient with us — continually providing His love, His comfort, His truth, and His power.

- *God's love is not based on our performance* (Romans 5:8). We may fall off the path of perseverance, but God's love has never been dependent on our actions, proven by the fact that He sent His son "while we were still sinners."

Yes, we are only one good choice away from being back on the path of perseverance. But no matter how far off the path or how long we are on it, God is patient with us and loves us as a dearly beloved child — part of His family (Romans 8:16 – 17; Galatians 4:7).

This reminds me of a touching story shared by my friend Karen Ehman, who lost over a hundred pounds in the first stage of her journey toward health. Her friend, Tammy, saw a "before" picture and was encouraging Karen enthusiastically when Karen's young son, Spencer, walked in. Tammy said, "Wow, Spencer, can you believe that was your mom? She's lost so much weight. Doesn't she look great?" In confusion, he looked back and forth between the photo and Karen and said, "Hmmm, they both look like Mama to me!"*

We are loved as God's special girls! No matter where you are in your struggle with healthy eating, God looks at you and says, "She still looks like my precious daughter to me!" He loves you just the way you are. But God loves you too much to leave you stuck in a state of defeat. You were made for so much more. You were made for victory.

Dear Lord, I am so thankful to be a part of Your family.
I know You love me no matter what. Please lead me today.
In Jesus' name. Amen.

---

*For more encouragement from my friend Karen Ehman, visit her at www.KarenEhman.com where she blogs daily.

DAY 2

Feeling Guilty?

For you created my inmost being;
you knit me together in my mother's womb.
I praise you because I am fearfully and wonderfully made;
your works are wonderful, I know that full well.

(PSALM 139:13 – 14)

Thought for the Day:
Sometimes I feel guiltier for what I'm not than thankful
for what I am.

I gathered the restaurant bags, sighed, and crammed them into the overstuffed trash can. A friend had sent me a recipe that day that involved peeling and chopping and simmering. I imagined her trash can full of fresh veggie peelings and other things that proved her kitchen produced way more homemade goodness than mine.

And a little thread of guilt wrapped around my heart.

Sometimes I feel guiltier for what I'm not than thankful for what I am.

But there was sweet grace waiting for me in a little yogurt shop that night. My daughter had asked if I would come and speak to a Bible study she was helping organize. "Mom, I think a lot of people are going to show up."

So instead of cooking that night, I ordered out. Again. And I drove to the yogurt shop with a girl whose heart was full of excitement and expectation.

People were everywhere. Young people. Invited people. And parents. Nearly two hundred people packed inside the yogurt shop and overflowed outside. My daughter smiled.

I took the microphone and spoke from my heart. I told my story. I taught truth. I invited the people to let Jesus be the Lord of their hearts.

And many who had never done so said yes to God that night. A teen girl who tried to commit suicide last year. She stood to accept Jesus. A young man with tears in his eyes. He stood to accept Jesus. A mom and a dad. They stood to accept Jesus. Along with many others.

In the yogurt shop.

With a woman whose trash can was filled with take-out bags and who isn't the greatest cook, but a woman who wants to learn to be more thankful for what I am than guilty for what I'm not.

Maybe you are the friend with the veggie peelings in the trash can and steaming homemade goodness on the table.

Celebrate that.

Or maybe you are like me. And your gifts are less tasty.

Celebrate that.

And cut the threads of guilt with the edge of grace.

Dear Lord, You made me in Your image—and that is something I seem to forget daily. Please help me remember to celebrate and live in who You made me to be, and not dwell on what I wish I were. In Jesus' name. Amen.

DAY 3

Why Do We Crave?

Do not love the world or anything in the world. . . .
For everything in the world — the lust of the flesh,
the lust of the eyes, and the pride of life —
comes not from the Father but from the world.

(1 JOHN 2:15 – 16)

Thought for the Day: While Eve focused on the object of her temptation, Jesus kept his focus on God's truth. What matters most to me?

Think about the definition of the word *craving*. How would you define it? Dictionary.com defines craving as something you long for, want greatly, desire eagerly, and beg for. God made us to crave so we'd always desire more of Him.

Don't read over that last sentence too quickly. God made us to crave — to desire eagerly, want greatly, and long for Him. But Satan wants to do everything possible to replace our craving for God with something else. I like how the New Living Translation puts this:

Do not love this world nor the things it offers you, ... for the world offers only a craving for physical pleasure, a craving for everything we see, and pride in our achievements and possessions. These are not from the Father, but are from this world. (1 John 2:15 – 16 NLT)

The cravings of the world are misplaced physical desires — such as issues with food or for sex outside of marriage. In other words, trying to meet our physical needs outside the will of God. A craving for everything we see means being enamored by material things. And lastly, pride in achievements and possessions describes someone chasing what brings feelings of significance.

This passage details three ways Satan tries to lure us away from loving God. And Satan used these very same tactics the first time he tempted humankind through Eve:

When the woman saw that the fruit of the tree was good for food [physical craving] and pleasing to the eye [material craving], and also desirable for gaining wisdom [significance craving], she took some and ate it. (Genesis 3:6)

Eve kept her focus on the object of her desire. The Scriptures give us no indication she tried to check in with God or Adam. She didn't walk away and truly consider this choice. And she certainly didn't take time to consider the consequences.

She saw it. She wanted it. She bought the lie. She took it. And she suffered for it.

Interestingly, Satan later applied the same three tactics he used with Eve when he tempted Jesus (Matthew 4).

Physical craving: Satan appealed to Jesus' physical need for food (Matthew 4:3). Jesus had been fasting, so of course He was hungry. It's comforting for me to know Jesus felt the pangs of hunger yet resisted because He was fasting. He didn't want to get His physical needs met outside the will of God.

Material craving: The devil promised Jesus all the kingdoms He could see if He would bow down to the god of materialism (Matthew 4:8–9). It's hard to resist the splendor of the world. But Jesus was enamored with God's eternity, not the world's temporary imitations. He didn't want to get His material needs met outside the will of God.

Significance craving: The enemy enticed Jesus to prove His significance by forcing God to command angels to save Him (Matthew 4:5–6). The lure of doing something that will make one look good, feel powerful, and be elevated in the eyes of others is so enticing. But Jesus' security came from His identity as a child of God, not His human achievements. He didn't want to get His emotional significance needs met outside the will of God.

While Eve focused on the object of her temptation, Jesus kept His focus on God's truth. He refuted each of Satan's lures with Scripture.

He saw it. He wanted God more. He quoted truth. He resisted. And He was rewarded for it.

When we face our own cravings, will we be like Eve, focusing on our object of desire? Or will we be like Jesus, pausing, reciting truth, and remembering what matters most? Temporary satisfaction or unending contentment? Giving in to the cravings of this world or following the love and the will of God? Two powerful examples. Two vastly different outcomes.

Dear Lord, please help me as I struggle with physical, material, and significance cravings. I know that only You can bring me lasting contentment for my cravings. Help me to pause today and reflect on what matters most. In Jesus' name. Amen.

DAY 4

Self-Control

Like a city whose walls are broken through
is a person who lacks self-control.
(PROVERBS 25:28)

Thought for the Day: The answer to keeping God's power with me and working in me to produce self-control is letting His Word get inside me.

Have you ever been in a discussion with a loved one when something snarky gets said and suddenly your blood pressure skyrockets, your nerves fray, and the worst version of you begs to come out?

Not that this ehhhhhver happens to me, of course.

Ahem.

Of course it happens to me. I live with other humans.

Whenever any kind of relationship conflict arises, my choice is whether to give the other person power to control my emotions.

When I react by yelling or flying off the handle or making a snappy comeback, I basically transfer my power to the other person. When I am void of power, I am void of self-control. So, it seems to me, if I'm going to remain self-controlled, I have to keep my power.

Now, when I say "my power," I don't mean something I conjure up myself. I am referring to God's power working in me. When I react according to God's Word, I feel that power. When I react contrary to God's Word, I feel powerless.

The prophet Isaiah provides a good reminder of what God Himself has said about tapping into His power, no matter what situation we are facing:

> "As the rain and the snow come down from heaven, and do not return to it without watering the earth and making it bud and flourish, so that it yields seed for the sower and bread for the eater, so is my word that goes out from my mouth: It will not return to me empty, but will accomplish what I desire and achieve the purpose for which I sent it."
>
> (Isaiah 55:10 – 11)

Did you catch that? The answer to keeping God's power with me and working in me to produce self-control is <u>letting His Word get inside me</u>. His Word seeping into my mind and my heart will accomplish things — good things, powerful things, things that help me display self-control.

So, all that to say, here's my new tactic: When I'm facing a situation where someone is getting on my last good nerve, I'm going to start quoting God's Word in the present tense. For example, if one of my sweet children starts acting *not so sweet*, I might say aloud (or silently, depending on the situation) words based on 1 Peter 5:6 – 8:

In this moment I'm choosing to be self-controlled and alert. Your actions are begging me to yell and lose control. I do have an enemy, but that enemy is not you. The devil is prowling and roaring and looking to devour me through my own lack of control right now. But I am God's girl. That's right, I am. I am going to humbly and quietly let God have His way in me right now. And when I do this, God will lift me and my frayed nerves up from this situation and fill me with a much better reaction than what I can give you right now. So give me just a few minutes and then we'll calmly talk about this.

Girl, that's some power right there.

And it will make you shine with so much self-control that your kids, your friends, your spouse, your coworkers won't know what to do with you.

Can you imagine what might happen if we wrote out powerful responses from God's Word on three-by-five cards and pulled them out every time we found ourselves in a situation? Take the first step by starting with one of the verses we've looked at today. Tuck that card away in your purse or put it someplace you will see it frequently.

I love being God's girl. Don't you?

Dear Lord, thank You that Your Word applies to so many areas of my life. Sometimes I really struggle with self-control and I need Your power to help me react in a graceful, godly way. In Jesus' name. Amen.

DAY 5

The Exploder Who Blames Others

Therefore be clear minded and self-controlled
so that you can pray.
(1 PETER 4:7)

Thought for the Day:
Feelings are indicators, not dictators.

Every now and then I attempt to be "that mom." You know, the one who wields a glue gun whilst craftifying something worthy of a showcase display at the Hobby Lobby. And the one who joyfully reads aloud to her children without being sneaky and skipping pages. Yes, her.

But it never works out for me.

Take, for example, the brilliant time I decided to attend a book warehouse clearance sale. I loaded up my kids and decided this was the perfect time to help my people fall in love with books. I wrongly figured a sale could help anyone feel the literary love. Not so.

My kids couldn't have cared less about the books.

What they wanted was in a crate off to the side of all the bookshelves. The brightly colored packages were laced with promises. I plucked from my kids' hands one that claimed to contain the coolest-ever science experiment. Anytime a brightly colored package uses the words *cool* and *experiment* on the front, a mother should beware. Especially when said package is marked down to one dollar. She should be very wise and tell her children, "No."

But, tired from all efforts to convince them to love books, I rationalized that since we'd dedicated our morning to this sale, we should at least walk out with something educational. So I bought several of the kits.

Sea monkeys. That's what the kits were supposed to grow. Key words: *supposed to*. My kids were beyond excited to get this party started. Into the container went the chemicals, the water, the little food crystals, and plastic green trees upon which the sea monkeys could play once they hatched.

It's at this point I should let you know that this is one of those good news/bad news stories. Yes, ma'am, which would you like first?

The good news ... something did hatch.

The bad news ... it wasn't sea monkeys.

After leaving the experiment overnight, I woke to find my kitchen invaded by the biggest, nastiest, hairiest giant flies you have ever seen. I'm not sure if our sea monkeys had a mutation situation going on or if some sort of larvae had gotten into the packages and eaten our sea monkeys.

Either way, it was awful.

The moral of this story is simple. Some moms are equipped by the hand of God to be "that mom." They have been formed with the three-C gene — Cooking, Crafting, and Cleaning come easily and naturally to them.

Others of us have been delightfully chosen to provide the comic relief necessary to keep this world entertained. And to keep future therapists in business.

I know this story sounds funny now, but at the time it was yet one more thing that excluded me from belonging to the good mom club. My internal good mom/bad mom dialogue tormented me:

Good moms grow sea monkeys. Bad moms grow nasty flies.

Wait! Good moms don't even buy sea monkey kits at a book sale. Bad moms struggle with telling their kids no and give in too easily.

Good moms get on the Internet and figure out how to turn a fly debacle into an enriching science lesson for their kids. Bad moms kill the stupid flies and hide all evidence of that from their kids.

And on and on the dialogue went. And with each assurance I was a bad mom, my emotions ratcheted higher and higher. On a stress scale from 1 to 10, I could have been hovering around 4, but then this conversation in my head pushed me all the way up to 7. Add to that a kid squabble over who licked whose toast at breakfast and the fact I couldn't find my cell phone, and I was all the way up to 9.8, ready to explode and blame anyone and everyone who had the misfortune to be nearby. What I felt was anger. What I needed was self-control.

I'm trying to better understand this whole concept of self-control. The Bible includes many verses about the subject, among them Proverbs 25:28, Galatians 5:23, and 1 Peter 4:7. But it's hard to display self-control when someone else does things out of my control that yank my emotions into a bad place. So here's a little tidbit I'm learning. When someone else's actions or statements threaten to pull me into a bad place, I have a choice. I do. It may not feel like

I have a choice. In fact, it may feel like I am a slave to my feelings — but I'm not. Remember, feelings are indicators, not dictators. Feelings can indicate there is a situation I need to deal with, but they shouldn't dictate how I react. I have a choice.

Dear Lord, when conversations, situations, and distractions in my day threaten to take over my emotions, please help me remember my feelings are indicators, not dictators. I want to quiet my inner dialogue and replace my anxiety with Your comfort and truth. In Jesus' name. Amen.

DAY 6

Compromise vs. Promise

"The thief comes only to steal and kill and destroy;
I have come that [you] may have life, and have it to the full."
(JOHN 10:10)

Thought for the Day: What happens when you take the "com" off of compromise? You are left with a promise. A promise you are meant to live.

I headed straight to the pantry. No doubt about it, this was an occasion when comfort food was completely justifiable.

My son had come to me scared and admitted that he had compromised his standards and gone too far with his girlfriend. They hadn't crossed every line, but enough that he knew they were headed in a dangerous direction. He wanted help processing what to do. We considered this definition:

com•pro•mise (kom´prə-mīz´)

1. to expose or make vulnerable

2. to make an unfavorable concession or indulgence

3. to weaken

This is exactly the way he felt—that they had exposed their relationship to emotions they were not ready to handle. They had indulged in an area God wanted to preserve, yet the world told them they deserved. And, it had weakened their relationship.

We sat on the back deck and processed the situation together. I said, "What happens when you delete 'com' from the word *compromise*? You're left with a 'promise.'" I shared that he was made for more than compromise. He was made for God's promises in every area of his life.

We read many of the empowering Scripture verses I've included in this book, seeking to filter every part of this situation through God's truth. In the end, he and his girlfriend came to the realization they needed to break up. It's really hard to put things in reverse after certain lines have been crossed.

I walked back into the house after that conversation with two things running through my brain. I was thrilled my son came to me to talk about such a sensitive issue. What an honor to breathe truth into his physical struggle.

But I also felt a little panicked at the realities of parenting an older teenager. And this feeling convinced me I had to have some comfort food! As I loaded my arms full of treats, I turned and saw my son standing on the other side of the kitchen. I was suddenly struck by a gut-wrenching question. How could I expect my son to apply truth to the area of his greatest physical struggle, but refuse to apply it to my area of greatest physical struggle?

This question struck deep. If I wanted to model what it looks like to live out truth in my physical struggles, I would have to break up with unhealthy choices. I admit that indulging in chips and brownies is a small concession compared to a young couple compromising their purity. But if one indulgence leads to two, and that leads to other indulgences, then the downward spiral is quite similar.

And whether we are talking about having premarital sex or other compromises that make us feel defeated, we must remember a crucial truth. We were made for God's promises that lead to an abundant life of truth, strength, and joy. Satan's purpose is to compromise God's promised best: "The thief's purpose is to steal and kill and destroy. My purpose is to give [you] a rich and satisfying life" (John 10:10 NLT). Don't allow this thief to weaken, expose, or make you vulnerable. Don't compromise. Refuse to accept less than the peace and abundant life God has promised you.

Listen for this lie the thief will often whisper: "This will make you feel wonderful!" Combat this lie with this: "You are a liar and a destroyer, Satan. Yes, this may feel wonderful in the moment, but how will I feel in the morning? I will not let your poisonous invitation for pleasure in the moment derail and defeat me. I am not made for compromise. I am made to live the reality of God's promises."

This is true for my son. This is true for me. This is true for you, dear friend.

Dear Lord, I know You will lead me to an abundant life of truth, strength, and joy. Protect me from the enemy's derailing distractions today. Help me to live out Your promises instead. In Jesus' name. Amen.

DAY 7

Rainy Days and Mondays

"Forget the former things; do not dwell on the past.
See, I am doing a new thing! Now it springs up;
do you not perceive it? I am making a way
in the wilderness and streams in the wasteland."

(ISAIAH 43:18 – 19)

Thought for the Day: The best thing for me to do is to position my heart in a place where I can experience God.

This devotion is for one of "those days." Yes, that kind.

If you're having a tough start to your day, I understand. Me too. I've been up since 3:00 a.m. and will seriously need some Holy Spirit empowering to make it until bedtime.

I'm tired. But I'm also feeling under attack. I know you know what I mean.

Satan typically throws everything he can at us to try to make us start off our days on an unglued footing. There will be kids who don't feel well. Marital tiffs. Unexpected demands that pop up on our to-do lists. Dogs that run away. And a mountain of laundry to be done.

And I just might have a little personal experience this morning with each and every item on that list. Lovely.

On days like this, I have to stand on what I know to be true instead of being whisked away in a sea of emotion. Here are three things I'm preaching to myself this morning:

1. I'm not a slave to my feelings. I'm the boss of them.
2. Just because I've had a few bad moments this morning doesn't make me a bad person.
3. This too shall pass. In the meantime, the best thing for me is to position my heart in a place where I can experience God.

And trust me, there is no better place to experience God than by opening His Word and then opening my heart to that Word. Which is exactly what I'm tempted to put off doing on an off-track day. But then I read a verse like our key verse: "Forget the former things; do not dwell on the past. See, I am doing a new thing! Now it springs up; do you not perceive it? I am making a way in the wilderness and streams in the wasteland" (Isaiah 43:18–19). See? God will make a way on this off-track day to put me and my unglued heart back on track.

I'm deciding to boss my feelings, realize bad moments don't define me, and look for the way God is already turning this day around.

Dear Lord, I want to remember that You are always here for me — on good days and bad. Help me to enjoy the good ones and receive Your help on the not-so-good ones. In Jesus' name. Amen.

DAY 8

But Victory Seems So Far Away

Rejoice always, pray continually,
give thanks in all circumstances;
for this is God's will for you in Christ Jesus.
(1 THESSALONIANS 5:16 – 18)

Thought for the Day: I can't control my circumstances, but I can control my choices. Setting mini goals — physically and spiritually — positions me for victory.

There are days I don't feel victorious. Like the day when the upstairs toilet clogged and flooded my kitchen ceiling. Or the day I got stuck in traffic, yelled at my kids, and missed an important meeting. Those are the days when my long-term goals to get healthy don't feel as important as my need for immediate comfort. I just want to blow my healthy eating plan out of frustration with something gooey, sweet, and cream laden.

I bet you've had something occur this week that doesn't make you feel very victorious either. A sick child, a missed deadline, tension in a friendship, or a number on the scale that almost made you cry. I understand. But may I encourage you? Even in the midst of trying circumstances and bad days, you can be victorious.

You can be victorious even when the distance between your present reality and your desired goal seems so far apart.

How?

Set mini-goals. Losing twenty, fifty, one hundred pounds, or more can seem so far away. And faraway goals are hard to hang onto when life drains us and it feels like those French fries sure could fill us.

Set mini-goals physically by getting a strategy for making healthy choices. How can you prepare now to drink eight glasses of water today? What is a healthy snack option you'll turn to when those afternoon salty and sugary cravings start calling? Are you going out to eat at a restaurant? Use the Internet to look up the nutritional information for their menu so you can make informed healthy choices. If hit with an unexpected temptation today, what healthy go-to script or Bible verse can you arm yourself with in advance to combat justifications and compromises?

Each mini-goal you accomplish today is a moment of victory.

We can also set mini-goals spiritually. We will always be most victorious when we are in the center of God's will. When we are in God's will, we are able to see our trials from God's perspective —through the lens of His grace and truth. But what is God's will?

The apostle Paul wrote, "Rejoice always, pray continually, give thanks ... for this is God's will" (1 Thessalonians 5:16 – 18). This is an explicit description of what God's will is. To be in the center of God's will is to be a woman who is joyful, prayerful, and thankful.

Be joyful: Intentionally look around for measures of joy each day. There is joy in simply being alive and in being redeemed by

God. Remember, joy is a choice we make, not a feeling we hope to get from our circumstances. It's good to look for the good, to celebrate it even in small ways. Doing so is a moment of victory.

Be prayerful: Focus your thoughts on God through prayer. When I was tempted with unhealthy choices, it used to trigger a pity party. Now, I turn my temptations into triggers to pray. Turning to God rather than turning to food is a moment of victory.

Be thankful: When I focus on how much weight I still need to lose, it brings me down and I start entertaining thoughts of defeat. However, when I focus on all that I'm gaining with God through this process of losing the weight, it makes me all the more determined to keep going. What is something positive you've gained during your weight loss journey so far? God's activity can be seen much more readily when we focus on what we do have rather than what we don't have.

We can't control our circumstances, but we can control our choices. Setting mini-goals physically and spiritually positions us for victory today. Indeed, *you can be victorious* even when the distance between your present reality and your desired goal seems so far apart.

Dear Lord, help me to remember that no matter how far away my goal may seem, I am most victorious when I am in the center of Your will. Today I will intentionally look for Your joy as I pray out of a thankful heart. In Jesus' name. Amen.

DAY 9

The Curse
of the Skinny Jeans

*For he chose us in him before the creation
of the world to be holy and blameless in his sight.*
(EPHESIANS 1:4)

Thought for the Day: Tying our happiness to food, skinny jeans, relationships, or anything else sets us up for failure. But tying our security, joy, and identity to God's love is an anchor we can cling to no matter what our circumstances may be.

Once I reached my goal weight, I thought I'd never have a bad day again. I mean really, what could possibly trouble me if I could fit into my skinny jeans? Boy, was I wrong.

A hurtful email . . . a disrespectful attitude from one of my kids . . . a missed appointment . . . a messy house . . . a stressful situation at work . . . an unexpected bill. Here I was just hours after feeling thrilled at finally being able to wear my skinny jeans, falling prey to the same topsy-turvy stuff I used to think wouldn't bother me if only I were smaller.

This is the curse of the skinny jeans.

The painful truth I've had to accept is that my body size is not tied to my happy. If I was unhappy when I was larger, I'll still be unhappy when I get smaller.

For years, I tied happiness to my circumstances and my hopes for the future. I thought, "I'll be happy when my father comes back, when I get married, when I have kids, when the economy improves, when I lose those extra pounds." But even when some of those things came true, I was still dissatisfied. Surely, there was more to me than my circumstances.

One day, I read a list of Bible verses that describe who God says I am, no matter the circumstances in my life, good or bad. I took that list of Scriptures and started to redefine my identity. It was a stark contrast to the way I'd been defining myself. I finally realized that things like my circumstances or what other people think don't define me. Instead, I could tie my happiness to the reality of who my heavenly Father says I am:

- Lysa, the forgiven child of God (Romans 3:24)
- Lysa, the set-free child of God (Romans 8:1–2)
- Lysa, the accepted child of God (1 Corinthians 1:2)
- Lysa, the holy child of God (1 Corinthians 1:30)
- Lysa, the made-new child of God (2 Corinthians 5:17)
- Lysa, the loved child of God (Ephesians 1:4)
- Lysa, the confident child of God (Ephesians 3:12)
- Lysa, the victorious child of God (Romans 8:37)

We were made to be free, holy, new, loved, and confident in who God made us to be. Because of this truth, we can't allow our minds to partake in anything that negates our real identity. Tying our happiness to food, skinny jeans, relationships, or anything else will only set us up for failure. But tying our security, joy, and identity to God's love is an anchor we can cling to no matter what our circumstances may be.

Dear Lord, I declare today that I was made to be free,
holy, new, loved, and confident in who You made me to be.
Protect me from anything today that challenges this truth.
Help me to redefine my identity. In Jesus' name. Amen.

DAY 10

Comparisons Stink

Each of you should use whatever gift
you have received to serve others,
as faithful stewards of God's grace in its various forms.
If anyone speaks, they should do so
as one who speaks the very words of God.
If anyone serves, they should do so
with the strength God provides,
so that in all things God may be praised
through Jesus Christ. To him be the glory
and the power for ever and ever. Amen.

(1 PETER 4:10 – 11)

Thought for the Day: Only when I get out of the shadow of doubt can I move into the life-giving reality of who God made *me* to be.

Okay, can I just be brutally honest about something? Comparisons stink. They do.

Just when I think I've gotten to a good place in some area of my life, along comes someone or something else that's better. And my confidence just shrinks back, takes the hand of doubt, and starts ransacking the peace right out of my heart and mind. Yes, there are Scriptures that can help with this. And yes, God can use it for good in my life. But honest to goodness, it's hard on a girl's heart.

Recently, I was put in a situation where something I feel very vulnerable about was held up to another person's near perfection. I was on a beach vacation with several friends who have dancer's legs. And by dancer, I mean like twenty-year-old, ballerina-perfection legs. I guess you could say I have dancer legs too if you are referring to the dancing hippo from *Madagascar*. I can eat healthy and exercise every bit as much as my ballerina friends, but long, lean legs just aren't in my genetic makeup.

So there I was on the beach. My weakness standing beside their strength. My yuck placed next to their glory. And in the private space of my most inner thoughts, I cried. And even more than that, I found myself feeling defeated and convinced this area won't ever be a strength of mine. I wasn't designed for this to be my strength.

Oh, I can make progress, for sure. And heaven knows, I do work on it. And on my good days, I see how God is using this all for good. But when comparison sneaks in, it can be hard. Worse than hard. It can just quite simply make me forget all the strengths I do have. And when I forget, my hearts shifts. I stop being thankful and instead become consumed by that little thing I don't have. What a dangerous place to be.

When I was struggling recently, I later realized I wasn't prayed up. I had not asked God to help keep my focus on Him. I just found myself wallowing—and wallowing isn't of the Lord. Amen? Amen!

I share this because you need to know—I struggle. Just like you. I'm on a journey of learning. Just like you. And I desperately need God's truth to bump into my weaknesses every single day. Only then can I get out of the shadow of doubt and into the life-giving reality of who God has made *me* to be. And see it as good. Not perfect. Not even close. But good. And good is good.

God, thank You for teaching me today to find my identity in You and to stop the difficult game of comparison. I know as I focus on who I am in You, jealousy won't be the thing that makes me become unglued. Amen.

DAY 11

I Need to Be Honest about My Issues

Search me, God, and know my heart;
test me and know my anxious thoughts.
See if there is any offensive way in me,
and lead me in the way everlasting.

(PSALM 139:23–24)

Thought for the Day:
Avoiding reality never changes reality.

Mostly I'm a good person with good motives, but not always. Not when I just want life to be a little more about me or about making sure I look good. That's when my motives get corrupted.

The Bible is pretty blunt in naming the real issue here: evil desires.

Yikes. I don't like that term at all. And it seems a bit severe to call my unglued issues evil desires, doesn't it? But in the depths of my heart I know the truth. Avoiding reality never changes reality.

Sigh. I think I should say that again: Avoiding reality never changes reality. And change is what I really want.

So upon the table I now place my honesty: I have evil desires.

I do.

Maybe not the kind that will land me on a *48 Hours Mystery* episode, but the kind that pull me away from the woman I want to be. One with a calm spirit and divine nature. I want it to be evident that I know Jesus, love Jesus, and spend time with Jesus each day. So why do other things bubble to the surface when my life gets stressful and my relationships get strained? Things like . . .

Selfishness: I want things my way.

Pride: I see things only from my vantage point.

Impatience: I rush things without proper consideration.

Anger: I let simmering frustrations erupt.

Bitterness: I swallow eruptions and let them fester.

It's easier to avoid these realities than to deal with them. I'd much rather tidy my closet than tidy my heart. I'd much rather run to the mall and get a new shirt than run to God and get a new attitude. I'd much rather dig into a brownie than dig into my heart. I'd much rather point the finger at other people's issues than take a peek at my own. Plus, it's just a whole lot easier to tidy my closet, run to the store, eat a brownie, and look at other people's issues. A whole lot easier.

I rationalize that I don't have time to get all psychological and examine my selfishness, pride, impatience, anger, and bitterness. And honestly, I'm tired of knowing I have issues but having no clue how to practically rein them in on a given day. I need something simple. A quick reality check I can remember in the midst of the everyday messies.

And I think the following prayer is just the thing:

God, even when I choose to ignore what my heart is saying to me, You know my heart. I bring to You this [and here I name whatever feeling or thoughts I have been reluctant to acknowledge]. *Forgive me. Soften my heart. Make it pure.*

Might that quick prayer help you as well? If so, stop what you are doing—just for five minutes—and pray these or similar words. When I've prayed for the Lord to interrupt my feelings and soften my heart, it's amazing how this changes me.

Dear Lord, help me to remember to actually bring my emotions and reactions to You. I want my heart reaction to be godly. Thank You for grace and for always forgiving me. In Jesus' name. Amen.

DAY 12

Honestly

Be diligent in these matters;
give yourself wholly to them,
so that everyone may see your progress.
(1 TIMOTHY 4:15)

Thought for the Day: It is possible to rise up, do battle with our issues, and, using the Lord's strength in us, defeat them — spiritually, physically, and mentally — to the glory of God.

I think we all get to a place sometimes where we have to honestly assess, "How am I doing?"

It's not really a conversation I have with a friend or family member. It's one of those middle-of-the-night contemplations where there's no one to fool. There's no glossing over the realities staring me in the face.

I know certain things about myself need to change, but it's easier to make excuses than tackle them head on. Rationalizations are so appealing:

I'm good in every other area.

I make so many sacrifices already.

I need comfort in this season of life—I'll deal with it later.

I just can't give this up.

The Bible doesn't specifically say this is wrong.

*It's not really a problem; if I wanted to make a change, I could—
I just don't want to right now.*

Oh for heaven's sake, everyone has issues; so what if this is mine?

And on and on and on.

Excuses always get me nowhere fast. That's why a few years ago I had to get honest in the area of healthy eating. Even if that's not your issue, I suspect these same scripts of rationalization have played out in your mind over other things.

So, the cycle continues day after day, week after week, year after year.

One day, I finally decided I didn't want to spend a lifetime in this cycle.

Nothing changed until I made the choice to change. I had to want it—spiritually, physically, and mentally. The battle really is in all three areas.

Spiritually: The Bible tells us to set our minds and our hearts on things above (Colossians 3:1–5). To do this, I have to put to death whatever belongs to my earthly nature, which is anything that sets itself up as an idol in my life. Idolatry is trying to get my needs met outside the will of God.

I couldn't deny it. This described food for me at times. More often than I cared to admit, I turned to food when I should have turned to God.

Physically: I couldn't keep my weight stable in a medically healthy range for any period of time. I would lose weight, but then I would always gain it back. And then to top it all off, when a doctor did some tests to determine my body mass index (BMI), my body fat percentage had crept up to the "danger" category.

What?! I knew I was feeling sluggish and frustrated by the extra weight, but no one would have looked at me and thought I was at risk. Except now a doctor was telling me that if I didn't make some changes, I could be in trouble.

I needed a healthy eating plan, not a fad diet. I needed a plan that would help me make realistic changes to improve my overall health and help me shed the excess weight the right way.

Mentally: Don't settle. Don't compromise. Remember what we discussed in Day 9 about cutting the "com" off of the word *compromise*? You're left with a "promise." We were made for more than compromise. We were made for God's promises in all areas of life. I am made for more than a vicious cycle of eating, gaining, stressing; eating, gaining, stressing . . .

For the sake of my emotional health, it was time to be honest with myself.

Remember, as a Jesus girl, it is possible to rise up, do battle with our issues, and, using the Lord's strength in us, defeat them — spiritually, physically, and mentally — to the glory of God.

Dear Lord, help me to be courageous enough to speak honestly to You and to myself about areas where I'm giving in to compromise. Show me how to rely on Your strength for more self-discipline in my life — not for my glory, but for Yours. In Jesus' name. Amen.

DAY 13

More than Feelings

Search me, God, and know my heart;
test me and know my anxious thoughts.
See if there is any offensive way in me,
and lead me in the way everlasting.

(PSALM 139:23–24)

Thought for the Day: We can't look to our feelings to determine truth. We must look to truth to rein in our feelings.

A few months ago I was speaking at a banquet where I met a precious young woman in her early twenties. She sheepishly made her way over to me with tears welling up in her eyes. She looked around before she whispered, "I don't feel saved. I have asked Jesus to be my Savior more times than I can count, but I just don't feel anything. What am I doing wrong?"

She wasn't doing anything wrong.

She was just looking in the wrong direction. She was looking for some magical feeling to swoop across the broken places of her life and instantly make everything feel different. That's not the way it works.

We can't look to our feelings to determine truth. We must look to truth to rein in our feelings.

Feelings are fickle. Feelings change on a whim. Feelings are paper thin and incapable of remaining untainted, unbiased, and unchanging. Faith can't be built on what we do or do not feel.

Truth, on the other hand, is stable, solid, and certain.

In the kindest way, I bossed her feelings with some truth. "You said you believe Jesus is the Savior, and you've confessed that with your mouth. You've asked Him to be the Lord of your life and for forgiveness of your sins. Right?"

She nodded, her eyes glistening with sincerity.

"Then park your mind, your heart, and your feelings on that truth and by the power of Jesus reject any lie that comes against that truth. You are saved. You are a child of God. You are eternally secure. Now, walk in that truth."

A wave of relief swept over her face. She threw her arms around me and buried her face in my jacket. I knew she was getting a little snot on my shoulder, and I could not have cared less.

I was too busy letting my own little sermonette make its way to my heart. I hadn't been doubting my salvation, but I had been doubting something else. I had been feeling afraid about releasing the message of *Made to Crave*.

After all, you can mess with a lot in a woman's life, but if you start messing with her food—that's grounds for serious irritation.

What if people didn't feel like embracing the message? What if people didn't feel like changing? What if it was just my issue and no one else really needed this message? What if people read it and remained unaffected and unchanged? What if I started backsliding in this area and made God look bad?

We can't look to our feelings to determine truth. We must look to truth to rein in our feelings.

I whispered these words over and over and over until they reached those raw places of insecurity deep in my soul.

Even if every single one of those feelings came to pass — people rejected the message and I gained my weight back — it wouldn't change or negate the absolute truths in the message. And it certainly wouldn't make God look bad. God doesn't build the stability of His identity on the fragile choices of His children. He just keeps placing the truth in front of us and offers to lead us to His best — over and over and over.

Dear Lord, I know I cannot look to my feelings to determine truth. I must look to You. Help me to be led by Your truth. Remove any doubts from my mind and lead me to freedom. In Jesus' name. Amen.

DAY 14

Gentleness Is in Me

Let your gentleness be evident to all.

(PHILIPPIANS 4:5)

Thought for the Day: The more I rejoice, the more I keep things in perspective. The more I keep things in perspective, the gentler I become.

Lately, I've had this Bible verse chasing me around: "Let your gentleness be evident to all" (Philippians 4:5). I've run across this verse in so many unexpected places that I know it's something God wants me to pay attention to. Why? Let's just say, when the Lord was handing out the gentleness gene in July of 1969, I was apparently in another line waiting for something else. Lots of people who were being fashioned at the same time did get the gentleness gene. I know some people who I'm sure stood in line twice and got a double portion. Me? Not so much.

Now, I can have moments of gentleness. I can perform acts of gentleness. But gentleness doesn't ooze from the core of who I am. This is especially true if I am sleepy or stressed. Honestly, I think I need one of those warning signs on the bedroom door to enter at your own risk after 8:30 p.m.: "DANGER! Please note that the Holy Spirit has temporarily left this woman's body to go help a sister halfway around the world who is just now waking up."

Now, I know that is some terrible theology, but I'm being honest, y'all. What little threads of gentleness I do have are not evident past 8:30 p.m. Not. At. All.

And then there is this thing that happens when I get stressed. Normally, I can pull off a little gentleness throughout the day, but throw in a stressful situation where too much is coming at me too quickly and mercy lou! I get task-oriented and start talking in a staccato-like cadence to my people, because I want the stuff around the house done. right. now. not. in. ten. minutes. because. now. means. now!

I don't want this to be how my kids remember me. Staccato mama.

I don't want this to be how *I* remember me in this season of life.

So this Philippians verse that has been nipping at the edges of my heart and mind, about letting my gentleness be evident to all, is something I know I need—even if it does sting a bit.

Here's a little sermon I've been preaching to myself: Let *your* gentleness be evident to all. The "your" part means I do have some. Much as I'd like to believe otherwise, God didn't skip over me in distributing the gentleness gene, and my wildfire personality isn't a divine exception. Regardless of the stress I'm under, I am capable of displaying God's gentleness because the Holy Spirit is in me. I have the Holy Spirit in me when I feel all chipper at 8:30 a.m., and I have the Holy Spirit in me when I feel grumpy at 8:30 p.m. The Spirit is in me when I feel calm and when I feel stressed. Gentleness is in *me*!

I just have to learn to reclaim the gentleness that is rightfully mine.

And I can reclaim it by practicing the one word that appears right before "Let your gentleness be evident to all" (Philippians 4:5). That little word is *rejoice*: "Rejoice in the Lord always. I will say it again: Rejoice!" (Philippians 4:4). The more my heart is parked in a place of thanksgiving and rejoicing, the less room I have for grumpiness.

My kids are driving me crazy? At least they are healthy enough to have that kind of energy. Don't miss this chance to rejoice.

My laundry is piled to the ceiling? Every stitch of clothing is evidence of life in my home. Don't miss this chance to rejoice.

My husband isn't all skippy romantic about the two of us shopping together? In the grand scheme of life, so what? He's a good man. Don't miss this chance to rejoice.

I feel unorganized and behind and late on everything? Scale back, let unrealistic expectations go, and savor some happy moments today. Don't miss this chance to rejoice.

The more I rejoice, the more I keep things in perspective. The more I keep things in perspective, the gentler I become.

That's why I have to intentionally seek out perspective-magnifying opportunities. Things like serving at a soup kitchen, delivering gifts to a family in need, or going on a mission trip. If I want the gentleness inside me to be unleashed, I have to break away from my everyday routine. I have to go where perspective awaits me.

Dear Lord, some days I just don't feel gentle. But I do want to obey Your Word. So right now, I ask You to help me change my perspective and walk in the gentleness You have given me. In Jesus' name. Amen.

DAY 15

I Want Legs Like Hers

A heart at peace gives life to the body,
but envy rots the bones.
(PROVERBS 14:30)

Thought for the Day: Every situation has both good and bad. When I want someone else's good, I must realize that I'm also asking for the bad that comes along with it.

If you're like me, chances are you've struggled with comparison and envy. Her stomach is flat; I've got a muffin top. Her hips are narrow; mine give new meaning to the word *curvy*. Her legs are long and lean; mine are like tree trunks.

Suddenly, all my blessings pale in comparison. What I *don't have* blinds me from seeing what I *do have*. My heart is drawn into a place of misguided assumptions and ingratitude … as I assume everything is great for women who possess what I don't have and I become less and less thankful for what is mine.

And here's the real kicker … things for the person I'm comparing myself to are almost never what they seem. If there's one lesson that living more than forty years has taught me, it's that everybody has not-so-great aspects to their lives. Whenever I get an idyllic view of someone else's life, I often say out loud, "I am not equipped to handle what they have, both good and bad."

God has had to teach me a lot about how to nip a comparison in the bud so it doesn't develop into full-blown envy and jealously. The statement, "I am not equipped to handle what they have, both good and bad," has been one of the greatest gifts God has given me. Every situation has both good and bad. When I want someone else's good, I must realize that I'm also asking for the bad that comes along with it. It's always a package deal. And usually if I'll just give something enough time to unfold, I often thank God I didn't get someone else's package.

One of the first times I came to understand this truth was in middle school when I met a beautiful girl at the children's theater in my town. We were both budding child actors cast in a Christmas play. During rehearsals, I remember seeing her long dancer's legs move in ways my stubby limbs never could. Her legs were muscular, lean, and graceful. Mine couldn't be described with any of those adjectives.

One day this girl had unusual pain in her left leg. A doctor's appointment turned into a battery of tests that turned into a hospital stay that turned into a diagnosis. Cancer. A surgery to remove a tumor turned into an amputation that turned into a complete life change. Her world was filled with words no child should ever have to know: chemotherapy, prosthetics, hair loss, and walking cane.

As a young girl, I was stunned by the whole experience. Especially because I clearly remember asking God for legs exactly like hers night after night as I watched her glide across the stage.

I was not equipped to handle what she had, both good and bad.

I don't want to paint the picture that every good thing someone else has will end with a tragedy. That's not the case. Sometimes others' good things are simply fantastic. But they are fantastic for them — not me.

I love the truth of Proverbs 14:30: "A heart at peace gives life to the body, but envy rots the bones." Sitting around wishing my legs were shapelier did nothing but discourage me and make me feel rotten. However, getting out and exercising made me come alive. It wasn't a quick fix and I still can't say I have dancer's legs, but I have peace knowing I'm doing what I can. And it is good.

Dear Lord, thank You for entrusting me only with what I have and who I am. Help me take my focus off what others have. Instead, help me make the best of what I've been given. My body is a gift. A good gift. In Jesus' name. Amen.

DAY 16

Getting Unstuck
from My Thinking Rut

Do not conform any longer to the pattern of this world,
but be transformed by the renewing of your mind.
Then you will be able to test and approve what God's will is —
his good, pleasing and perfect will.

(ROMANS 12:2)

Thought for the Day:
We won't develop new responses
until we develop new thoughts.

Brain research shows that every conscious thought we have is recorded on our internal hard drive known as the cerebral cortex. Each thought scratches the surface much like an Etch A Sketch. When we have the same thought again, the line of the original thought is deepened, causing what's called a memory trace. With each repetition the trace goes deeper and deeper, forming and embedding a pattern of thought. When an emotion is tied to this thought pattern, the memory trace grows exponentially stronger.

We forget most of our random thoughts that are not tied to an emotion. However, we retain the ones we think often that have an emotion tied to them. For example, if we've had the thought over and over that we are "unglued," and that thought is tied to a strong emotion, we deepen the memory trace when we repeatedly access that thought. The same is true if we decide to stuff a thought — we'll perpetuate that stuffing. Or if we yell, we'll keep yelling.

We won't develop new responses until we develop new thoughts. That's why renewing our minds with new thoughts is crucial. New thoughts come from new perspectives. The Bible encourages this process, which only makes sense because God created the human mind and understands better than anyone how it functions.

A foundational teaching of Scripture is that it is possible to be completely changed through transformed thought patterns. That's exactly the point of today's key Scripture. Scripture also teaches that we can accept or refuse thoughts. Instead of being held hostage by old thought patterns, we can actually capture our thoughts and allow the power of Christ's truth to change them:

> We demolish arguments and every pretension that sets itself up against the knowledge of God, and we take captive every thought to make it obedient to Christ. (2 Corinthians 10:5)

I don't know about you, but understanding how my brain is designed makes these verses come alive in a whole new way for me. Taking thoughts captive and being transformed by thinking in new ways isn't some New Age form of mind control. It's biblical, and it's fitting with how God wired our brains.

I can't control the things that happen to me each day, but I can control how I think about them. I can say to myself, "I have a choice to have destructive thoughts or constructive thoughts right now. I can wallow in what's wrong and make things worse, or I can ask God for a better perspective to help me *see* good even when I don't *feel* good." Indeed, when we gain new perspectives, we can see new ways of thinking. And if we change the way we think, we'll change the ways we act and react.

Jesus, teach me to trust You and to believe that even though my situation is overwhelming, You are out to do me good. Give me Your perspective today. Amen.

DAY 17

Pinches and Grace

Let us then approach God's throne
of grace with confidence,
so that we may receive mercy and find grace
to help us in our time of need.
(HEBREWS 4:16)

Thought for the Day:
Today is a beautiful time for grace.

I wanted to pinch the two girls sitting on the front row of our church service. Pinch them, I tell you. But they were five rows ahead of me, and my arm couldn't quite reach. Since I couldn't physically get their attention, I prepared my "look." You know, the one that says a thousand corrective statements with just a cross expression and a raised eyebrow? Yes, that one.

The minute one of them stole a glance in my direction, they were gonna know exactly how I felt about their wiggling and obvious lack of attention during the service. Oh, and might I mention, these two girls belonged to me. Well, at least one of them did. The other was my daughter's friend, who sometimes goes to church with us.

I don't think anyone else really noticed them. They weren't being disruptive to other people. But they weren't acting the way I wanted them to. I wanted them sitting up straight, drinking in the message, and taking pages of notes. Thank you very much.

Suddenly, an annoying little thought started to tug at the corners of my mind. *You want your children to act perfectly because it makes you look good. Let that go. They don't need to be sitting up straight, furiously taking notes, to hear God's message. This is a beautiful time for grace. And when you give grace ... you won't come unglued.*

Ouch.

I don't much like the Holy Spirit speaking to me the kind of truth that hurts. I was in the mood to pinch somebody. Two somebodies. Give grace? Now? It wasn't what I wanted, but it was exactly what I needed to do in that moment.

Soon my daughter's friend peered back to look at me. Despite my feelings, I made the choice to smile, wink, and give her a little wave. Then this wiggly, usually not-very-affectionate middle schooler got out of her seat, walked back the aisle five rows, threw her arms around me, and gave me a hug that preached a thousand sermons right then and there.

Indeed, grace was exactly what was needed in that moment.

And that's what makes this parenting thing so stinkin' hard. There are really no textbook answers. Only God can prepare me with the wisdom and discernment necessary for each and every potentially unglued parenting moment.

It's such a moment-by-moment balancing act of loving, shepherding, disciplining, extending grace, molding, modeling, loving some more, and maybe having to give a few pinches along the way too.

God, I pray that today You would give me the strength to stay close to You to experience Your grace and give Your grace. Open my eyes to the challenging situations around me that need a dusting of Your grace. Amen.

DAY 18

How Does Your Garden Grow?

Commit to the LORD whatever you do,
and he will establish your plans.

(PROVERBS 16:3)

Thought for the Day: I wanted the flowers, but not the work. Isn't that the way it is with many things in life?

One spring, I took a new route through our neighborhood and caught a glimpse of a man hard at work in his glorious flower garden. I've often looked at other people's flowers and secretly wished for my own lush display. However, the glimpse of this man with his hands digging deep into the earth brought a new revelation. He had a garden because he invested time and energy in cultivating it. He didn't wish it into being. He didn't hope it into being. He didn't just wake up one day and find that a garden of glorious blooms had miraculously popped up from the dirt.

No. He had a goal. He had a plan. He worked at it. He sacrificed for it. It took intentionality, sweat equity, determination, and consistency. And it took time and patience before he ever saw any fruit from his labor. But eventually, there was a bloom ... and then another ... and then another.

I saw this man's flowers and wished for my own—without a clue about all the work that had gone into producing them. I wanted the flowers, but not the work. Isn't that the way it is with many things in life? We want the results, but have no idea where to start or how much work will be required.

In addition to wishing for a garden, I also spent many years wishing for a thinner body. I had lost weight before, but I couldn't keep it off for any extended time. I was lax about actually changing what I ate, and I excused away the necessary discipline. Then I'd catch myself wishing I were thinner and making excuses about my age and metabolism, decrying the unfairness of my genetic disposition, blah, blah, blah. My changes were based more on wishful thinking than action. They were also always temporary; therefore my results were also temporary.

Consider these verses in the book of Proverbs, God's gift of wisdom and practical guidance to his people:

> The plans of the diligent lead to profit as surely as haste leads to poverty. (21:5)

> Commit to the LORD whatever you do, and he will establish your plans. (16:3)

When it comes to personal growth in how we care for our health, we need to move beyond wishful thinking. Consider the demands of your daily life and choose a healthy eating plan with reasonable goals based on sound medical advice. Commit your actions—your eating plan and food choices—to the Lord. Then you will reap results not just on the outside, but inside your heart where joy and peace will take root and blossom.

Dear Lord, thank You for these verses in Proverbs. I want to feed on Your truth today. I commit to turn my focus to You. Help me to plan well, work hard, and sacrifice with intention. In Jesus' name. Amen.

DAY 19

The War against My Soul

Dear friends, I urge you,
as foreigners and exiles, to abstain from sinful desires,
which wage war against your soul.
(1 PETER 2:11)

Thought for the Day: Being ruled by anything other than God is something He takes quite seriously. And so should we.

For years, I refused to think of my struggle with healthy eating as anything more than just a physical issue. I didn't pray about it. I didn't apply biblical insights to it. And I certainly didn't ask God for help. I just wallowed in my lack of self-control.

This issue was too small for God, but too big for me.

When I began connecting my physical struggle with spiritual insight, I wasn't convinced that God really cared about my bulging body. Was I merely being vain to want to be thinner? Was I wasting my time on things of this world when I went to the gym? Was I just a foolish, Jesus-chasing girl who mistakenly believed my desires to please Him with this food battle would somehow help me grow closer to Him?

As I studied the Scriptures, I knew I had my answer from God: "Dear friends, I urge you, as foreigners and exiles, to abstain from sinful desires, which wage war against your soul" (1 Peter 2:11).

My ever-increasing weight and poor food choices were wreaking havoc on my body. But that wasn't all. My desperate struggle, hopelessness, and uncontrollable food cravings were waging war against my soul. These were some of the whispers being hissed in my ear: *You'll never be free from this battle. You will always bounce from feeling deprived when you're dieting to feeling guilty when you're splurging. Victory isn't possible!*

When Satan holds up food in front us and says these things, we must see that an inappropriate relationship with food can be the lure he uses to draw us away from God. Satan may also use alcohol, unedifying media, inappropriate friendships, overspending, or any other means to lead us into a place where we feel self-control isn't possible. He's not choosy about the method, just the result.

One day while reading Psalm 23, I listed all the things the Lord does for me:

- He leads me.
- He restores me.
- He guides me.
- He is with me.
- He comforts me.
- He fills me.
- He satisfies me.

As I read back over my list, a series of questions shocked me: Do I rely on the Lord in these ways or do I rely on food in these ways? Do I honestly turn to God or turn to food? Do I seek to be comforted, filled, and satisfied in the depths of my soul with God, or food? My answers made me cry.

Being ruled by anything other than God is something He takes quite seriously. And so should we. For years, I was overweight physically but underweight spiritually. Tying those two things together has finally allowed me to see why so many other diets failed. I needed to dig past the surface to the real heart and soul of my issues.

In the process of that soul digging, I realized how amazing it is to serve a compassionate God—a God who knew food would be a major stumbling block, keeping many of His children from wholeheartedly pursuing Him. So He's given us great gifts in the Holy Spirit, Jesus, and the Bible to help us.

Start and finish your day with Bible reading. Pray before you eat—even snacks. Listen to that spiritual gut check when you're about to eat something. Choose the healthy option. Stop before you're overly full. Eat slowly. Refuse to stuff and gorge. Stay on a slower eating pace while enjoying conversation with others.

Yes, I want to get healthy. Yes, I want to lose weight. But this journey is about so much more. In the end, pursuing health helps my heart to feel closer to Jesus and more ready to receive what He wants for me each day.

Dear Lord, it is true. My food struggles at times wage a war against my soul. Because of this one overwhelming struggle, I often feel defeated in other areas of my life as well. As I seek You today, please give me the strength I need. Thank You. In Jesus' name. Amen.

DAY 20

Real Problems

Discretion will protect you,
and understanding will guard you.
(PROVERBS 2:11)

Thought for the Day: It's good to know the difference between an inconvenience and a real problem.

I will face issues today that I could think of as problems. I might be tempted to call them problems. They will bother me as if they are problems. I will feel these situations are truly problematic.

But they aren't — not in light of what others are facing today. Real problems. Life-altering problems. Problems that will still sting a month from now, a year from now, ten years from now. My friend Jade battling cancer, hoping to live long enough to see her daughter graduate from high school, is a problem. My daughter forgetting to get a permission slip signed and my having to run up to the school to take care of it is an inconvenience — not a problem.

Indeed, I'll have hard things to face today. I'll have things that make me sad today. I'll have setbacks and interruptions and inconveniences I will deal with today. But not problems.

Oh, that I would know the difference. And when I come to the realization that what I have aren't really problems, I can look at my hard things and see they aren't so hard after all.

I can look at the things that make me sad today and choose to be a little less sad. I can face setbacks without getting set back. I can be interrupted and choose to look for God in the midst of it all. Because I know what real problems are. And what I have aren't those.

I think it's good to know the difference between an inconvenience and a real problem. Don't you?

Dear Lord, thank You for gently leading me toward a perspective change. Help me to recognize the difference between an inconvenience and a real problem. And no matter which one I'm facing, I want to respond according to Your Word. In Jesus' name. Amen.

DAY 21

The Friendship Challenge

*Perfume and incense bring joy to the heart,
and the pleasantness of a friend springs
from their heartfelt advice.*
(PROVERBS 27:9)

Thought for the Day: Establishing real intimacy with a friend requires pushing past the resistance, the fear, and our unglued reactions.

What makes a woman tender also reveals her vulnerabilities.

What makes a woman transparent also exposes her wounds.

What makes a woman authentic also uncovers her insecurities.

And there isn't a woman alive who likes being revealed, exposed, and uncovered. But to establish real intimacy with a friend requires pushing past this resistance, past the fear, and past our unglued reactions. To be known is to risk being hurt.

Friendship is risky. But friendship can be beautiful.

I want you to think about a friend in whom you can make an investment this week. I challenge you not to think of the friend with whom you feel most comfortable. Rather, think of the friend who might benefit from seeing a little more of your tenderness, transparency, and authenticity.

There is someone in your sphere of influence who feels desperate to know that someone else understands.

Might you take three days and give her three friendship investments?

Day 1: Have a conversation with her in which you honestly admit one of your vulnerabilities or insecurities. Chances are, she'll reveal something of herself to you as well. Then commit, really commit, to praying for her.

Maybe wear your watch on the opposite wrist. Every time you're distracted by this out-of-sorts placement, use it as a prompt to pray for your friend. Think of the burden she's been carrying lately and carry it in your prayers this day.

Day 2: Buy this friend a gift—just because. It doesn't have to cost much, but make an investment of time to think of something that would really be delightful to her.

Day 3: Write your friend a note to attach to the gift. In the note, tell her at least three things you admire about her and acknowledge some way she's made a difference in your life. Then deliver this little just-because gift and note to your friend. This friend who sometimes feels a little vulnerable. Wounded. Exposed in some way.

Your honesty and thoughtfulness will be such a sweet investment —for her, for you, for your friendship.

Being vulnerable in a friendship is a great way to pave the road to the kind of honesty that keeps our relationships healthy.

Are you up for taking the friendship challenge?

Dear Lord, thank You for the friends you have given me and thank You for this sweet reminder today. Help me to expose those vulnerable, hard-to-reach places with my friend. I want to show Your love through this challenge. In Jesus' name. Amen.

DAY 22

Afternoon Acts
of Kindness

Teach me your way, LORD,
that I may rely on your faithfulness;
give me an undivided heart, that I may fear your name.
I will praise you, Lord my God, with all my heart;
I will glorify your name forever.
(PSALM 86:11 – 12)

Thought for the Day: What if I could be courageous enough to act and react like a complete person — a Jesus girl who is filled, sustained, and directed by God's joy?

I'll admit, loving incomplete people doesn't seem like the obvious path to joy. And it doesn't seem like an obvious topic to be covered in a book on getting healthy and keeping our skinny jeans in proper perspective. But stick with me here, you might be surprised.

Just the other day I was pondering some of those distressing emails I mentioned earlier, and I reached the conclusion that incomplete people are a trigger that make me want to eat. They are complicated and sensitive and messy in their reactions. They have the potential to drain my resolve and make me grumpy.

The last thing I want to do when a person throws their incompleteness in my direction is love them. I want to grab a bag of Cheetos and rationalize how much a treat is certainly in order right now. Then I want to sit on my couch and tell the air around me how much I love Cheetos and how much I dislike incomplete people.

But what if I dared in that moment to think differently? What if I could be courageous enough to act and react like a complete person—a Jesus girl who is filled, sustained, and directed by his joy? Instead of looking at this incomplete person's offense, what if I could see the hurt that surely must be behind their messy reaction?

I pause. I don't reach for the Cheetos. I don't react harshly out of my own incompleteness. I don't wallow in my thoughts of how unfair and unkind this other person is. And I choose to love instead … taking out a piece of stationery and responding with words of grace, or crafting an email with a message of compassion.

Better yet, what if I were to do this every afternoon, even when I haven't had a run-in with an incomplete person but am just simply craving things I shouldn't eat? I've been trying this out lately and I love it. Afternoon acts of kindness are yet another unexpected but beautiful result of letting Jesus direct my healthy eating pursuits.

Each day I've been asking Jesus who in my life needs words of encouragement, and He always puts someone on my heart. So, instead of filling my afternoons with thoughts of frustration toward others or tempting thoughts about food, I am filling my afternoons with His thoughts of love toward others. And this is a great place to be, no matter if I'm wearing my skinny jeans or not.

After all, the ultimate goal of this journey isn't about making me a smaller-sized person but rather making me crave Jesus and His truths as the ultimate filler of my heart. We are to remain in this healthy perspective.

Let His thoughts be our thoughts. Remain.

Let His ways be our ways. Remain.

Let His truths go to the depths of our hearts and produce good things in our lives. Remain.

Approach this world full of fellow incomplete people with the joy of Jesus. Remain.

And see our skinny jeans as a fun reward, nothing more. Remain.

And be led forth in peace because I've kept my happy tied only to Jesus. Remain.

Dear Lord, I want to be courageous enough to act and react like a complete person today. Please help me to see areas where I need to change and grow. I desire to crave You and Your truths more than anything else because You are the ultimate filler of my heart. In Jesus' name. Amen.

DAY 23

Because I Am Loved

Humble yourselves, therefore,
under God's mighty hand,
that he may lift you up in due time.
(1 PETER 5:6)

Thought for the Day: Doing something in order to be loved is a trap, but doing something because I am loved is incredibly freeing.

My friend Kathrine Lee once said to me, "The first time I lost weight, I did it *so that* I'd be loved—and I gained all the weight back. This time around I'm losing weight *because* I am loved, and it's made all the difference in keeping the weight off." The truth of her statement struck me profoundly. And it applies to so much more than just weight loss.

Doing something so that we'll be loved is a trap many of us can get caught in. When I do something because I'm trying to get someone else to notice me, appreciate me, say something to build me up, or respect me more, my motives get skewed. I become very me-focused. I put unrealistic expectations on myself and the other person. And I can get stinkin' angry when I don't feel adequately noticed, appreciated, or respected.

But doing something because I am loved is incredibly freeing. Instead of looking at a relationship from the vantage point of what I stand to *gain*, I look instead at what I have the opportunity to *give*. I am God-focused and love-directed. I keep my expectations in check. And I am able to lavish on others the grace I know I so desperately need. I live free from regret, with clarity of heart, mind, and soul.

The apostle Paul wrote, "But now let me show you a way of life that is best of all. If I could speak all the languages of earth and of angels, but didn't love others, I would only be a noisy gong or a clanging cymbal" (1 Corinthians 12:31b – 13:1 NLT). And you want to know what chips away at the security of knowing I am loved? The noisy lies of the enemy. He has no love in him; therefore his voice is useless.

Are your efforts toward your goal hounded by clanging thoughts of inadequacy, fears of rejection, and hopelessness? Reject those clamorous thoughts and replace them with the love thoughts that God has sent our way through the ages:

Humble yourselves, therefore, under God's mighty hand, that he may lift you up in due time. Cast all your anxiety on him because he cares for you. Be alert and of sober mind. Your enemy the devil prowls around like a roaring lion looking for someone to devour. Resist him, standing firm in the faith, because you know that the family of believers throughout the world is undergoing the same kind of sufferings. And the God of all grace, who called you to his eternal glory in Christ, after you have suffered a little while, will himself restore you and make you strong, firm and steadfast. (1 Peter 5:6 – 10)

Isn't it interesting how much easier it is to apply Scripture when we're doing it because we're loved? Consider how this applies to the passage from 1 Peter:

Because I am loved, I can humble myself. When I'm trying to be loved, I must build myself up to look better.

Because I am loved, I can cast all my anxiety on Him. When I'm trying to be loved, I cast all my anxiety on my performance.

Because I am loved, I resist Satan and stand firm in my faith. When I'm trying to be loved, I listen to Satan and stand shaky in my feelings.

Because I am loved, I know God will use trials to make me stronger. When I'm trying to be loved, I wonder why God would allow trials.

Indeed, I want to pursue my goals — health and otherwise — from the vantage point of my friend Kathrine. *Because I am loved.* That's when my motives stay pure and my heart stays grounded in the comfort and assurance of God's never-changing love.

Dear Lord, I don't want my motives to get skewed during my healthy eating journey. Help me to not be me-focused in this process. I long to be God-focused because I am loved by You. Thank You. In Jesus' name. Amen.

DAY 24

Soul Rest

"Come to Me, all who are weary and heavy-laden,
and I will give you rest. Take My yoke upon you
and learn from Me, for I am gentle and humble in heart,
and you will find rest for your souls.
For My yoke is easy and My burden is light."
(MATTHEW 11:28–30 NASB)

Thought for the Day:
Where there is a lack of Sabbath rest,
there is an abundance of stress.

I was in the kitchen the other day with my teenage son. He was stirring a pot of rice and I was sorting through the day's mail. It was a rare, quiet moment in my house when all the other kids were gone, so I wanted to make the most of an opportunity to connect with him.

"Mark, what are you thinking about?"

"Nothing," he replied. And I knew from the gentle way the word slowly tumbled out, it wasn't a brush-off. But how in heavens could he be thinking about nothing? I had to know.

"So when you say nothing, do you really mean nothing? Or do you mean you are thinking about something you don't want to tell me about?"

"No," he said. "I mean I'm really not thinking about anything right now."

"How is that possible?" I asked. "Like, you don't have one thing you are worried about or a conversation you're rehashing or a bunch of lists you are mentally reviewing in your mind?"

He tilted his head and looked at me like I was one giant unplucked eyebrow. "Ummm ... nope."

Amazing. Truly amazing. And challenging. I think I need to be a little more like Mark when it comes to emotional white space. Although he may be wired with the ability to easily enter into a place of mental rest, God is calling me to incorporate more times of rest into my life. I desperately need them.

Rest sounds so good, but it is difficult for a girl like me. Even when my physical body is at rest, my mind rarely is. Can you relate?

It's tough. And yet the Bible makes it very clear that we are to make time for rest. More than just physical rest, we need to take a spiritual and emotional rest from going our own way — literally. Once a week, we are to hit the pause button on life and guard a day of rest for our souls. Guard it fiercely and intentionally — even if the demands on our schedules beg us not to.

This is hard for me. I'm not good at pausing and letting my soul enter into Sabbath rest. I haven't come close to mastering this and I am far from being a Sabbath heroine. But I am a messenger who has been trying to make some imperfect progress in this area. Because I know where there is a lack of Sabbath rest, there is an abundance of stress. And where there is an abundance of stress, there is great potential for me to eventually come unglued.

Father, finding rest in my busy life often seems impossible. But I am a woman desperate to find this place of rest. Please open my heart to find this place where You so long to renew my life each week. Amen.

DAY 25

The Exploder Who
Shames Herself

Finally, brothers and sisters, whatever is true,
whatever is noble, whatever is right, whatever is pure,
whatever is lovely, whatever is admirable — if anything
is excellent or praiseworthy — think about such things.

(PHILIPPIANS 4:8)

Thought for the Day: Sip the shame so you won't have to guzzle gallons of unwanted regret.

The first line of the email was "Shame on you."

Lovely.

It was from a fellow middle school parent who was deeply offended that her daughter hadn't been invited to my daughter's birthday party. Take note of two words in that last sentence that strike fear deep within the hearts of many, many mothers: *middle school.* Need I say more? Glory be.

Never mind that Hope had been having problems with this girl hurting her feelings all year. Never mind we'd decided to invite only the girls in her homeroom class, of which this girl was not part. And never mind we wished we could invite this girl, but the fear of her repeating the hurt she'd caused in school sent Hope into a crying fit.

So we didn't invite her. I'm not saying this was the right decision. But honestly, it wasn't done out of spite at all. We'd done so many things to reach out and extend love to this girl, and Hope was just completely worn out from continually getting nothing but hurt back. It was a tough decision and one I didn't make lightly.

But, still, I got this email. Not only did I get the shame-on-you email, but this other mom was clear about her plans to have Hope called into the principal's office and reminded to be kind to her daughter.

I don't know what the official definition of a *twit* is. Nor am I completely sure *twit* is a real word. However, when you feel all twisted up, with irritation sprinkled on top, *twit* seems fitting.

So there I was in a twit right at the start of a new day.

Typically, I am a middle school parent who stays out of the drama. And I readily admit when my kids need to be corrected and redirected. But on this day I could envision myself zinging the person who hurt me with the perfect comeback. I mentally weighed all the many reasons I was perfectly justified in leveling the scales of hurt.

She dumped a bucket of hurt on me. The scale tipped heavy on my side. Therefore, I should dump a bucket of hurt on her. Then the scales would be even and my twit would dissipate in this balance of hurt equality. But something in my spirit didn't feel any better after I mentally walked through this leveling of the scales.

I felt heavy.

In this instance, I was about to be an exploder who would later feel shame for not acting more like someone who really loves Jesus and follows Him. Being able to identify my tendency helped me see in advance the downside of the reaction I was about to have. I imagined myself feeling the shame of exploding on this woman and I didn't like how it felt. I didn't want shame to be my reality.

I'll sometimes say to myself, "Sip the shame so you won't have to guzzle the regret." In other words, taste a little bit of the shame of what will be if you let it all rip before you find yourself drowning in gallons of unwanted regret.

Sipping the shame of what would be if I let my raw emotions have their way helped me not to explode. And that's good. But I still had some processing to do to get the hurtful feelings to dissipate. The last thing we want to do is trade our unhealthy exploding for unhealthy stuffing. Remember, the balance between the two is soul integrity where our honesty is godly.

Dear Lord, thank You for Your patience as I try to make progress with my reactions. Please help me to be truly honest but full of grace with those You have put in my life. In Jesus' name. Amen.

DAY 26

Desperation
Breeds Defeat

No temptation has overtaken you
except what is common to mankind. And God is faithful;
he will not let you be tempted beyond what you can bear. . . .
He will also provide a way out so that you can endure it.
(1 CORINTHIANS 10:13)

Thought for the Day: Desperation does indeed breed defeat. But God promises answers for desperate situations.

I was walking through the airport when an incredible aroma suddenly grabbed my attention and taunted, *Do you know how happy I can make you?* A candy shop had just made a fresh batch of nutty, caramel popcorn.

There's nothing wrong with caramel popcorn except that it definitely wasn't on the healthy eating plan I'd committed to. I felt my knees get weak because I love caramel popcorn. I started to rationalize buying this special treat, thinking, "I can't get this at home, and I'll take half home to my kids. What harm will a little caramel popcorn do?" I felt an extreme gravitational pull straight to the object of my desire.

The only thing that stopped me was redirecting my thoughts away from the popcorn and onto a new truth God had been teaching me: desperation breeds defeat. This truth was the perfect match for my temptation and helped me walk away.

The book of Genesis tells an interesting story about twin brothers who illustrate this point. The elder son, Esau, was favored by his father, Isaac, because of his prowess as a hunter. In contrast, the younger son, Jacob, was a quiet homebody.

One day, Esau returned home from an unsuccessful hunting trip totally famished and demanded some stew from his brother. "I'll give you food," agreed Jacob, "but first, trade me your birthright."

"Okay," Esau replied, "I'm so hungry, I'm about to die." So Esau traded the honors due to him as the firstborn son for a simple meal of stew.

On first glance, it's easy to ridicule Esau's decision. I cannot imagine selling my whole birthright for a pot of soup. But I had to look at my own life and ask, "What great thing have I traded for so little in return? How often do I trade healthy food for junk food? What temporary pleasure have I craved so much that I gave up lasting victory?"

Desperation does indeed breed defeat. But God promises answers for desperate situations. The "way out" that God provides is the ability to decide in advance what I will and will not eat each day.

I plan my meals right after breakfast when I'm feeling full and satisfied. The absolute worst time for me to decide what I'm going to eat is when I've waited until I'm depleted and feeling hungry. So I prepare a healthy snack to have on hand or keep in my purse.

When I'm unprepared or I've rushed through a proper meal, my stomach screams for something quick. And quick options usually come in a variety of unhealthy temptations, just as I experienced at the airport. However, that day I had decided ahead of time that I would keep an apple in my purse for a snack, rather than trade my healthy progress for something like caramel popcorn.

If we purposely think and plan before we eat, we'll be better able to see the "way out" that God promises when we are tempted — and to keep our cravings centered on God alone.

Dear Lord, I acknowledge that I need You. I need You in my times of desperation, and I also need You in times of jubilation. Help me to think ahead so I won't be weak when I am faced with temptation. In Jesus' name. Amen.

DAY 27

The Very Next Step
You Take

Just as you used to offer yourselves
as slaves to impurity and to ever-increasing wickedness,
so now offer yourselves as slaves to righteousness
leading to holiness.

(ROMANS 6:19)

Thought for the Day: Victory isn't a place we arrive at and then relax. Victory is when we pick something healthy over something not beneficial for us — again and again.

When I'm at my lowest emotionally, even I don't want to follow my own advice. I don't want to "be made new in the attitude of [my] mind" (Ephesians 4:23), nor do I want to "put on [my] new self, created to be like God in true righteousness and holiness" (Ephesians 4:24).

What I want to do is cry. I want to withdraw. I want to be jealous that others don't have my issues. I want to be mad at God for giving me this metabolism. And I want my very next choice to be high in calories, fried in fat, and iced with something that makes my taste buds sing.

I want victory, but I feel so weak.

This hardly sounds like someone who has conquered her food issues, right? The reality is, even when we stand on the scale and see our goal weight staring back at us, we're always just one choice away from reversing all the progress we've made.

I'm not saying victory isn't possible. It is. But victory isn't a place we arrive at and then relax. Victory is when we pick something healthy over something not beneficial for us. And we do it again. And again. We maintain our victories with each next choice.

Here's a biblical perspective from the apostle Paul:

> I put this in human terms because you are weak in your natural selves. Just as you used to offer the parts of your body in slavery to impurity and to ever-increasing wickedness, so now offer them in slavery to righteousness leading to holiness. (Romans 6:19 NIV 1984)

You see, the very next choice we make isn't really about food, weight, or even the negative feelings we carry around when we're choosing poorly. It's about whether or not we're positioning ourselves for holiness — to live the kind of God-honoring lives in which, by God's strength, sustained discipline is possible.

So how does one tap into God's strength? Certainly with prayer. Definitely through Bible reading. But there's another part to it. We tap into God's strength by practicing the gentle art of balance.

God's holy people knew there was a time to feast, a time to fast, and a time for simple daily nourishment. That's what it means to practice balance. If I understand balance, I will eat to live — not live to eat. I will enjoy nourishment, not gorge on empty calories. I will eat until satisfied, not eat to be satisfied. As Romans 6:19 says, I will make right choices that honor God and lead to holiness rather than constant indulgences that lead to defeat.

Whether the struggle is a food issue, a moral issue, an emotional issue, or a relationship issue, deep down you know when something is pulling your heart away from God. Deciding to live in a place of sustained discipline means making the choice not to view a struggle as an inevitable curse, but rather to see it as something good — something from which to learn and grow stronger. And, one good choice later, you will taste the empowerment of true balance and continue reaching forward from there.

Dear Lord, I am challenged to ponder what is pulling my heart away from You. Help me to live in a place of balance and to embrace what You have for me today. In Jesus' name. Amen.

DAY 28

Plan for It

Therefore put on the full armor of God,
so that when the day of evil comes,
you may be able to stand your ground,
and after you have done everything, to stand.
(EPHESIANS 6:13)

Thought for the Day: It's God's promises — His truths and examples from Scripture — that are powerful enough to redirect us to the divine nature we're meant to have.

Once, while traveling, I experienced a vivid illustration of how crucial it is to have predetermined procedures. I had taken my seat on a flight to a speaking engagement. Everything seemed to be quite normal during the rest of the boarding process, but as the plane was about to taxi, things got very abnormal. A woman just a few rows behind me started screaming obscenities. And when I say screaming, I don't mean talking too loudly. I mean full-out vocal extremes.

She was completely undone because she found a piece of chewed gum stuck to her bag of chips. Where the gum came from was a mystery, but how she felt about that gum was not. What came out of her mouth was so R-rated it made my already wide eyes pop out like a bug on steroids.

She was so loud and out of control that the flight attendants quickly alerted the captain to abort the flight. When it became obvious the flight attendants were not going to be able to contain the situation, two plainly dressed men on the plane suddenly stood and flashed federal marshal badges.

One of the marshals gathered the flight crew while the other went to talk to the woman. Every airline professional on board immediately went into by-the-book mode. It was clear they had been well trained on how to handle crazy situations. They didn't get emotional or come unglued in any way. They simply followed procedures. I watched in amazement as the woman kept escalating her wild behavior, but the people trained to handle her never did.

She screamed.

They talked in calm, hushed tones.

She threatened.

They deflected her threats with gentle warnings.

Then she took things to a whole new level: "I have a bomb! I have a bomb! I have a bomb!"

I am not kidding.

I know you think I am. But I am not.

That's when I pulled out the anointing oil my pastor had given to me the day before. My seat became oily and holy. I called Art and my friend Amy and asked them to pray. And I tweeted, asking my cyber friends to pray.

Eventually, the marshals — along with two policemen and additional Homeland Security people who'd boarded the plane — handcuffed her and removed her from the flight. Throughout the whole hair-raising debacle, I never once heard the people following procedures yell or come unglued even one tiny bit. And I was absolutely amazed.

I will be honest with you: This woman took unglued to a level I hope I never experience again. But I also never want to forget the incredible responses of the flight attendants and officers who dealt with this explosive situation. Not only did their obviously thorough training and procedures keep them calm, they kept an entire planeload of passengers calm as well. And that was an amazing thing to behold.

So, I started thinking that maybe I needed a set of default procedures for when selfishness, pride, impatience, anger, and bitterness rear their ugly heads. Because in the moment I feel them, I feel justified in feeling them and find them hard to battle.

We'll explore my predetermined plan in the next five devotions, but for today, remember it's God's promises — His truths and examples from Scripture — that are powerful enough to redirect us to the divine nature we're meant to have. How do you want to display God's divine nature working in you the next time you feel a little unglued? I want to be calm, levelheaded, and show evidence of loving Jesus. What about you?

Dear Lord, thank You for Your divine power to help me stay out of the emotional fray. Please keep me anchored to the divine nature I am meant to have. In Jesus' name. Amen.

DAY 29

If Only We Knew

For we do not have a high priest
who is unable to sympathize with our weaknesses,
but we have one who has been tempted in every way,
just as we are—yet was without sin.
Let us then approach the throne of grace with confidence,
so that we may receive mercy and find grace
to help us in our time of need.

(HEBREWS 4:15–16)

Thought for the Day: One drop of the Lord's mercy is better than an ocean of the world's comfort.

Here is my prayer for you today: *May you catch even the slightest glimpse of the tender mercy of our Lord Jesus. For one drop of the Lord's mercy is better than an ocean of the world's comfort.*

The marriage situation that seems impossible.

The finances that never balance.

The hope so deferred it makes your heart sick.

The anxiety over a child bent on a wayward path.

The diet you are sick of.

The broken promises of a friend.

The lack of true friends.

The constant messiness always distracting the peace you want in your home.

The impatience and frustration, anger and disappointment of losing it — again.

If only we knew how deeply Jesus understands and cares for us. If only we could see the wonder of His love. The skies He paints, the flowers He blooms, the world He arranges just for us. The love letters He's written to us throughout the Bible.

These are all mercies from Him.

The world will offer us comfort in the form of escapes. We escape to romance novels, movies, magazines, malls, chocolate, vacations, affirmations from friends. Not that any of these things are bad. They aren't. But they are very temporary. They make us feel good in the moment, but that good never stays. We need more and more. Trying to fill our aching hearts with these things is like trying to fill an ocean with a tablespoon. It's never enough. So we clench our fists and keep trying to find something to comfort us.

If only we knew how to stop clenching our fists so that we could open our hands and catch the drops of His tender mercy. If only we knew how to release the weight of trying to fix it all ourselves. If only we knew to stop in the midst of it all and whisper, "Jesus . . . help me." Just a whispered breath formed in the wholeness of His name carries all the power and mercy and wisdom and grace we need to handle what we face.

If only we knew.

If you find yourself wanting to escape today into one of the world's comforts, first invest some time in asking Jesus to help you, show you, and direct you. Specifically, ask Him to help you see and notice His tender mercies. Then you will see that, indeed, one drop of the Lord's mercy is better than an ocean of the world's comfort.

Jesus, I pray that today I would know how high and how deep is the love You have for me. Help me to catch the tender drops of Your mercy and allow myself to fully embrace Your love. Amen.

DAY 30

Knowing but Not Applying

Surely you desire truth in the inner parts;
you teach me wisdom in the inmost place.

(PSALM 51:6 NIV 1984)

Thought for the Day:
There is a big difference between ingesting and digesting.

It wasn't uncommon for me a few years back to read a diet book while mindlessly munching on chips. Or, curling up on the couch to watch *The Biggest Loser* with a bowlful of ice cream.

There is a big difference between ingesting and digesting.

Just taking in the inspiration of truth but never being transformed by it will lead you down a dangerous path of doubt. Doubting yourself. Doubting God. Doubting the effectiveness of truth.

And what a tragedy that is.

I should know. Too many times, I've been one to ingest without digesting: reading truth, but not applying it; liking a message I hear at church, but not living it; knowing what I must do to experience life change, but never putting it into action; taking in knowledge, but never letting it make a difference in my life.

Sweet sister, can we honestly admit together that we've all been there? And then can we agree together that we don't have to stay there?

When I initially posted these thoughts on my blog, I asked, "What is a healthy choice you have made recently or could make part of your life today?" The answers inspired me.

I am going to go grocery shopping and fill my fridge and cabinets with healthy options. It's amazing how much more healthy I eat when I plan to do so in advance. I'm actually excited about this!

My healthy choices are that I added fresh fruit and vegetables to my eating habits. I have also increased my water intake. It paid off—I lost 1.6 pounds this last week. Woo hoo! Healthier choices do make a difference.

My healthy choice for today was to get in another Zumba class this week!

My healthy choice for today is only eating when I'm truly hungry and not just "emotionally" hungry! Thanks for the article today. I needed the extra motivation.

I'm going to go run today. I want my body to get to the place where it craves exercise on a daily basis. Right now I have to work hard to motivate myself to get moving.

I have started using the treadmill. Today was the farthest I've ever gone—2.5 miles at 3.2 mph.

I keep saying, "I know what to do; it's just *doing* it that's the problem." I am eliminating sugar today. I have done this for almost two weeks, but yesterday chose to go my own way (ignoring all the principles I've learned and have been applying). So I'm steering back to the path He's having me walk. Thank You, Lord. I will digest, not just ingest!

What is a healthy truth you've been ingesting but not digesting? Why not let it sink deep? Start with just one thing. Maybe it's a physical choice, like drinking enough water. Or, maybe it's a spiritual choice, like believing you were made for more than this vicious cycle of defeat. Whatever it is, make progress there. Ingest that truth. Then digest it until it becomes part of who you are.

Dear Lord, I am inundated with information about how You want me to live. I hear Your truths at church, on the radio, in conversations with friends, when I read my Bible, and during Bible studies. These are all good things, but sometimes it feels overwhelming. Still, I want to do better. Forgive me for ingesting, not digesting Your truths. Help me to digest at least one truth a day so that I start living Your messages instead of just hearing them. In Jesus' name. Amen.

DAY 31

Sometimes We Just Have to Get Quiet

And the God of all grace, who called you to his eternal glory
in Christ, after you have suffered a little while,
will himself restore you and make you strong, firm and steadfast.
To him be the power for ever and ever. Amen.

(1 PETER 5:10 – 11)

Thought for the Day: I want to be a passionate woman reined in by God's grace — not an exploder who shames herself.

Remember that our goal, whether we are exploding and shaming ourselves or exploding and blaming others, is imperfect progress. When I've had an explosion, I feel a lot more *imperfect* than I do *progress*. We're dealing with emotions and relationships — both of which are like nailing Jell-O to the wall. It's a complicated, messy, and unpredictable process, for sure. Sometimes a girl can get worn out, wonder if she's ever going to really stop exploding, and feel like giving up.

But before I give up, I've learned to hush up. This often means hitting a pause button on whatever situation is making me feel like exploding. Ideally, this would mean getting away by myself in the quiet of my home. Sometimes this means excusing myself to the restroom. Bathroom stalls can make great prayer closets (smile). The point is that the only way I can see what God is doing and attend to what He reveals is to get quiet with Him.

Here are five beautiful things I've discovered in the quiet with God — straight from Scripture in 1 Peter 5:6 – 10. They are balm for the raw edges of a soul on the precipice of exploding.

1. In the quiet, we feel safe enough to humble ourselves.

The last thing I want to do in the heat of an emotional mess is to be humble. I want to be loud and proud and to prove my point. But I've learned the hard way that I have to step out of the battle and humbly ask God to speak truth to my heart in order for things to start making sense. Never have I had a relationship issue in which I didn't contribute at least something to the problem. Usually, I can only see this something in the quiet. The quiet is what enables us to "humble [ourselves], therefore, under God's mighty hand" (1 Peter 5:6).

2. In the quiet, God lifts us up to a more rational place.

When we are in the heat of a tangled mess, crazy emotions drag us down into a pit of hopelessness. The only way out of the pit is to make the choice to stop digging deeper and turn to God for a solution, so "that [God] may lift you up in due time" (1 Peter 5:6).

3. In the quiet, anxiety gives way to progress.

We can pour out our anxious hearts to Jesus, who loves us right where we are, just as we are. Because His love comes without unfair human judgment, we soften and feel safe enough to humbly admit we need Jesus to work on us. Trying to fix another person only adds to my anxiety. Letting Jesus work on me is where real progress happens. I claim the promise of 1 Peter 5:7: "Cast all your anxiety on him because he cares for you."

4. In the quiet, we acknowledge that our real enemy isn't the other person.

This person with whom we're in conflict may seem like the enemy and they might even look like the enemy. But the truth is, they aren't the real culprit. The real culprit is Satan, who is exerting influence on both me and the person offending me. I don't always realize this in the heat of the moment, but in the quiet, I can remind myself of the truth and choose a strategy for responding with self-control. That's the wisdom of Scripture, which says, "Be self-controlled and alert. Your enemy the devil prowls around like a roaring lion looking for someone to devour. Resist him, standing firm in the faith" (1 Peter 5:8–9).

5. In the quiet, I can rest assured God will use this conflict for good—no matter how it turns out.

If I make the effort to handle this conflict well, I can be freed from the pressure to make everything turn out rosy. Sometimes relationships grow stronger through conflict; other times relationships end. Because I can't control the other person, I must keep focusing on the good God is working out in me through this and leave the outcome with Him. God's Word promises that "the God of all grace, who called you to his eternal glory in Christ, after you have suffered a little while, will himself restore you and make you strong, firm and steadfast" (1 Peter 5:10).

Maybe you can add to this list as you discover your own benefits in getting quiet when all you really want to do is explode.

Imperfect progress.

Can you sense you're making your way toward this goal?

Oh God, help me. I want to be a passionate woman reined in by You and Your grace. I want to learn to hold my tongue and keep the Holy Spirit's power working in me. Help these truths sink in and become part of who I am and how I live. In Your sweet name. Amen.

DAY 32

Prayers Where
I Don't Speak at All

In the same way, the Spirit helps us in our weakness.
We do not know what we ought to pray for,
but the Spirit himself intercedes for us through wordless groans.
(ROMANS 8:26)

Thought for the Day: When we sit silent before God, the Spirit will intercede with perfect prayers on our behalf.

I had been going through some stinkin', rotten, horrible, no-good days and was at the absolute end of knowing what to pray. I'd slipped into a habit of praying circumstance-oriented prayers where I'd list every problem and ask God to please fix them. I even made suggestions for solutions in case my input could be useful. But nothing changed. Except my waistline and the amount of chocolate life suddenly required.

In a huff one day, I sat down to pray and had absolutely no words. None. I sat there staring blankly. I had no suggestions. I had no solutions. I had nothing but quiet tears and some chocolate smeared across my upper lip. Eventually, God broke through my worn-out heart. A thought rushed through my mind and caught me off guard: *I know you want Me to change your circumstances, Lysa. But right now I want to focus on changing you. Even perfect circumstances won't satisfy you like letting Me change the way you think.*

I didn't necessarily like what I heard during this first time of silently sitting with the Lord, but at least I felt I was connecting with God. I hadn't felt that in a long time. And so, to keep that connection, I started making it a habit to sit quietly before the Lord.

Sometimes I cried. Sometimes I sat with a bad attitude. Sometimes I sat with a heart so heavy I wasn't sure I'd be able to carry on much longer. But as I sat, I pictured God sitting there with me. He was there already, and I eventually sensed that. I experienced what the apostle Paul taught when he wrote, "In the same way, the Spirit helps us in our weakness. We do not know what we ought to pray for, but the Spirit himself intercedes for us with wordless groans" (Romans 8:26).

As I sat in silence, the Spirit interceded with perfect prayers on my behalf. I didn't have to figure out *what* to pray or *how* to pray about this situation that seemed so consuming. I just had to be still and sit with the Lord. And during those sitting times, I started to discern changes I needed to make in response to my circumstances —none of which included using food for comfort.

I think a lot of us try to get filled up with things or people. In *Becoming More Than a Good Bible Study Girl*, I talked about how I walked around for years with a little heart-shaped cup, holding it out to other people and things trying to find fulfillment. Some of us hold out our heart-shaped cup to food. Others demand that husbands love us in ways that right our wrongs and fill up our insecurities. Sometimes we expect our kids to be successful so that we look good and have our worth validated by their accomplishments. Or we overspend our budget on an outfit we just have to have.

Whatever it is, if we are really going to make lasting changes, we have to empty ourselves of the lie that other people or things can ever fill our hearts to the full. Then we have to deliberately and intentionally fill up on God's truths and stand secure in His love.

The more I fill myself up with the truths of God's love, the less I find myself pulling out that little heart-shaped cup. I have to mentally replace the lies with truth to remind myself of just how filling God's love really is.

Dear Lord, I often don't have words to pray. Remind me that as I'm silent before You, the Spirit intercedes for me. Please protect me from the lies that seem to creep into my mind at a moment's notice. Help me today, Lord, to keep my mind fixed on You. In Jesus' name. Amen.

DAY 33

One or Two Verses a Day

Alarmed, Jehoshaphat resolved
to inquire of the LORD.
(2 CHRONICLES 20:3A)

Thought for the Day: God's words are so rich, so penetrating, and so intentionally placed, I don't want to rush past a powerful few in an effort to get through a whole chapter.

Have you ever felt pressure to read more in order to have a better quiet time?

I don't think more always equals better.

Sometimes, truly, less is more.

For example, one of the messages I'm speaking at conferences right now is about King Jehoshaphat (2 Chronicles 20). I love the first three words of verse 3, "Alarmed, Jehoshaphat resolved ..." Right within those three words is a message that will preach—and should preach—to me all day long.

A message in three words, you ask?

Yes, ma'am.

I love how Jehoshaphat's name is book-ended in two opposite words.

"Alarmed" is how he was feeling.

"Resolved" is how he responded to his situation despite his feeling.

Jehoshaphat had just found out that three countries were banding together to fight against his smaller army. Yes, he should have felt alarmed. But what inspires me is his ability not to react out of his alarm. He stayed resolved, "resolved to inquire of the LORD." In other words, his feelings were an appropriate *indicator* of what he was facing but not a *dictator* for his reaction.

Here's the message that preaches to me: "My feelings should be an indicator of my situation but never a dictator of my reaction."

This applies to my eating and weight struggles. It applies to my relationship struggles. It applies to so many struggles.

I want to be resolved — resolved to inquire of the Lord. So, though my quiet time might consist of just three words, pondering how to be resolved will linger in my thoughts all day. And it will surely change my reactions, my words, and my thoughts.

How might the same thing happen when you unearth some of God's treasures tucked within just a few of His words? I've unearthed a lot of verses that relate to satisfying our deepest desire with God, not food. But there are more to be discovered. Find them! And then relate them to what you are facing today. Here are some great verses to get you started:

I lift up my eyes to the mountains — where does my help come from? My help comes from the LORD, the Maker of heaven and earth. (Psalm 121:1–2)

Jesus replied, "You do not realize now what I am doing, but later you will understand." (John 13:7)

In addition to all this, take up the shield of faith, with which you can extinguish all the flaming arrows of the evil one. (Ephesians 6:16)

They seldom reflect on the days of their life, because God keeps them occupied with gladness of heart. (Ecclesiastes 5:20)

Do not be afraid of them; the LORD your God himself will fight for you. (Deuteronomy 3:22)

By faith Noah, when warned about things not yet seen, in holy fear built an ark to save his family. (Hebrews 11:7a)

For it is God who works in you to will and to act in order to fulfill his good purpose. (Philippians 2:13)

What treasures did you discover among these Scriptures? Write them down and consider the individual meaning of each and the collective meaning of the statement as a whole. Then spend the day pondering the personal message God has for you.

Dear Lord, I love Your Word. I love the simple but very profound verses listed on this page. Help me to see You in each word. Help me to understand Your truth and to live it out today. I am Your child and I am dearly loved. Thank You, Lord. In Jesus' name. Amen.

DAY 34

Creating New Space
for Growth

Then [Jesus] said to them all:
"Whoever wants to be my disciple must deny themselves
and take up their cross daily and follow me."

(LUKE 9:23)

Thought for the Day: If I want to grow closer to God, I have to distance myself from whatever is distracting me.

Over the years, I have felt the desire to become more than just a checklist Christian. I've wrestled with the question, "How can I grow closer to God?" And I wasn't looking for the plastic Christian answers: Go to church. Read the Bible. Don't cuss. Be nice. Pray.

Those are all good things. Things we should do. But we can do all those things and still have hearts far from God. I want connection. I want communion. I want closeness.

The New Living Translation puts Jesus' words in Luke 9:23 like this: "If any of you wants to be my follower, you must turn from your selfish ways, take up your cross daily, and follow me." I want this kind of all-out pursuit with God. But what does this look like in today's culture?

I think part of what it means is breaking old habits to create space in my heart for new growth.

In reality, God desires our sacrifice — our turning from selfish ways — not for His benefit, but for ours. For instance, I stopped watching TV for a season. I realized I was turning on the TV when I felt most depleted — and when I'm most depleted, I soak up deeply whatever I take in. Why would I want to soak in deeply the entertainment of this world and not things that breathe life back into me? I broke the old habit of watching television and created space in my heart for new growth.

Another example is my commitment to do nothing else each morning — including checking my phone or turning on the computer — before I open up God's Word. I used to wake up eager to tune in to the world. I'd soon be sucked into answering this email, reading that Twitter post, and returning phone calls. Before I knew it, half my day was gone, and I hadn't let God prepare my heart for any of it. So I broke the old habit and created space in my heart for new growth.

Right now, I'm intentionally sacrificing sugar and processed foods that turn into sugar once consumed. Yes, I want to maintain my weight loss. But this journey is so much more than just that. It really is about learning to tell myself no and learning to make wiser choices daily. And somehow becoming a woman of self-discipline honors God and helps me live the godly characteristic of self-control. Giving up sugar was hard at first — really hard, like crying-big-crocodile-tears hard. But I broke the old habit and created space in my heart for growth.

Am I saying all my Jesus girlfriends need to do the same? No more TV? No checking your computer and phone first thing in the morning? No sugar? Nope. These aren't things I think everyone needs to do. They were personal practices for my own benefit. I'm not asking you to follow *me*; I'm saying to follow wholeheartedly after God. Ask Him. Seek Him. Do what He tells you.

If we want to grow closer to God, we'll have to distance ourselves from whatever is distracting us. Break the old habit and create space in your heart for new growth. And closeness will soon bloom.

Dear Lord, I realize that You do not need me. I need You. But I don't often live each day understanding this. Far too often, I forge ahead and battle my issues without You. I want to grow closer to You, to live each day with You. Help me to remember You will never leave me. Thank You for loving me. In Jesus' name. Amen.

DAY 35

A Deeper Purpose
for Exercise

Therefore, because of you
the heavens have withheld their dew
and the earth its crops.
(HAGGAI 1:10)

Thought for the Day: If we are really honest, we have to admit it:
we make time for what we want to make time for.

I found the most interesting story in the Old Testament about how
serious God is about people taking care of the temple entrusted
to them. Before the Holy Spirit was given to us and our bodies
became temples, the Spirit of God dwelt in such structures as a
portable, tent-like sanctuary called the tabernacle and the beautiful
temple originally built by King Solomon in Jerusalem.

During the time of the prophet Haggai, God's people had
returned from being in exile in Babylon. One of the first things
they set about to do was rebuilding the temple. They started with
great enthusiasm and wonderful intentions, but slowly slipped

back into complacency and eventually stopped their work on the temple altogether. Other things seemed higher priorities — more urgent, more appealing. Here is how Haggai describes it:

> This is what the LORD Almighty says: "These people say, 'The time has not yet come to rebuild the LORD's house.'"
>
> Then the word of the LORD came through the prophet Haggai: "Is it a time for you yourselves to be living in your paneled houses, while this house remains a ruin?"
>
> Now this is what the LORD Almighty says: "Give careful thought to your ways. You have planted much, but harvested little. You eat, but never have enough. You drink, but never have your fill. You put on clothes, but are not warm. You earn wages, only to put them in a purse with holes in it."
>
> This is what the LORD Almighty says: "Give careful thought to your ways. Go up into the mountains and bring down timber and build my house, so that I may take pleasure in it and be honored," says the LORD. (Haggai 1:2–8)

Oh, this reminds me just how divided my heart can be when it comes to taking care of my body — God's temple. Like these people, I could so easily say, "I'm not in a season where it's feasible to take care of my body. I just can't find the time between the kids, my work responsibilities, running a home, paying the bills, and all the day-to-day activities. It's just not realistic for me to exercise." But the Lord issues strong cautions to "give careful thought to [our] ways" and to make time to "build the house" so that he may be honored.

Note that God's people neglected rebuilding the temple for ten years. Each year something else seemed to be more important. That's the way exercise was for me. Year after year, something else always took precedence.

However, if I was really honest, I had to admit that I made time for what I wanted to make time for. I wasn't giving careful thought to my ways. I wasn't making a plan to exercise each day and giving that time the same priority as much more minor things. For example, I always seemed to find time to watch a favorite TV show or chat with a friend on the phone. Just the same, the Jews who returned from Babylon obviously had time to do things they really wanted to do as well. They found the time and energy to put paneling up in their own homes while ignoring the home of the Lord.

The Israelites suffered severe consequences for failing to care for the Lord's temple: "Therefore, because of you the heavens have withheld their dew and the earth its crops" (Haggai 1:10). Now, I'm not saying God will cause bad things to happen to us if we don't exercise. But there are natural consequences for not taking care of our bodies. People who don't care for their bodies now will live the consequences of those choices at some point. Whether it's more weight and less energy now or heart disease later, our choices matter both physically and spiritually. Spiritually, I feel much more weighed down by stress and problems when I'm not taking care of my body. Physically, I have less energy to serve God and more emotions to wade through when processing life.

I fully realize my temple may not be God's grandest dwelling, but I want to lift up to the Lord whatever willingness I have each day and dedicate my exercise as a gift to Him and a gift to myself.

Dear Lord, I want to care for my body in the ways I eat and in the ways I move. Help me to see the ability to exercise as a gift. I dedicate my temple to You and commit to start rebuilding it today. In Jesus' name. Amen.

DAY 36

The Most-Searched-For Answer

"I will instruct you and teach you
in the way you should go;
I will counsel you and watch over you."

(PSALM 32:8)

Thought for the Day: Salvation can't be found in anyone or anything else. There is no other. Only Jesus.

Growing up, I had a plan for how I could make my life good. Get a good education. A good job. A good husband. A few good kids. A good house. A good flower bed out front. And a good minivan parked in the driveway. Then life would be ... good.

Eventually, I had all that good stuff. And I was thankful for it all. I loved my family to pieces. The minivan wasn't all I thought it would be, but I felt like an official mom driving it. So even that wound up being good.

But something inside me still felt hollow. A little off. A little lacking. So, I reasoned, I needed something else to do. Something that would use my gifts and talents. And while these things were fun and satisfying on one level, they too fell short when it came to that deep place ringing with the echoes of empty.

Empty is a heavy load to bear. Wanting to be filled but not knowing what might fill the deep soul leaves a gnawing ache, prompting a search that can seem both futile and shattering at times.

When you try and try, always feeling like the answer is just around the corner, and then it isn't, your heart can split wide open and leak dry all your reserves.

It can make you feel unsatisfied and frustrated with everything. Even those you love. Maybe especially those you love.

So you fake a smile and keep putting one foot in front of the other. But eventually you stop peeking around the next corner hoping the answer is there. Past experience tells you it isn't. And wrapped in that perception is the noose that strangles hope.

Sadly, this is where many women live. I know this place because I lived there. I struggled there. "Salvation is found in no one else, for there is no other name under heaven given to men by which we must be saved" (Acts 4:12). We're not going to find something else to save us—only Jesus is equipped for that job.

No good plan is the answer. Even a good husband, good children, a good friend make a very poor God. No education or job or house can save you.

Salvation can't be found in anyone or anything else. There is no other.

Only Jesus.

And I'm not just talking about claiming to be a Christian. Following the rules and really following Jesus are two totally different things. Going through the motions of religion won't ever satisfy. True satisfaction comes only when we bend low, open our hearts in complete surrender, and say, "Jesus, it's you. Only you. There is no other."

And then we must really live like this is true.

Because it is. True.

Dear Lord, forgive me for trying to fill the empty places of my soul with people, possessions, and positions. I want to know what it means to have You, Lord, as the One who satisfies the deep longings of my heart. Show me. Teach me. Lead me. And I will follow. In Jesus' name. Amen.

DAY 37

The Underbelly

"This will result in your being witnesses to them.
But make up your mind not to worry beforehand
how you will defend yourselves. For I will give you
words and wisdom that none of your adversaries
will be able to resist or contradict."
(LUKE 21:13 – 15)

Thought for the Day: "Criticism may not be agreeable, but it is necessary. It fulfills the same function as pain in the human body. It calls attention to an unhealthy state of things." — WINSTON CHURCHILL

Criticism stinks. That's usually my first thought when someone makes it clear they don't like something I've done or said.

My pride says, "How dare you!"

My heart says, "I want a chance to explain."

My soul says, "Jesus, am I off base?"

My mind says, "Why do I open myself up like this?"

My feelings say, "Ouch."

Sometimes criticism is fair. Maybe I messed up and it would serve me well to reconsider. Other times criticism is nothing but rotten spew. And boy, does it stink. But if I get stuck in the stink, it serves no good purpose.

Might there be another way to look at harsh criticism? To get past the hurt to see if it has an underbelly I should consider?

The other day I Googled the word *underbelly* and stumbled on an article about the armadillo lizard. This fascinating creature has hard and pointy scales that have "Don't mess with me" written all over them. But, like all tough creatures, this lizard has a vulnerable place.

The armadillo lizard's tough exterior wraps around its back but softens at the underbelly. When threatened, the lizard grabs its tail and displays a prickly, intimidating posture to keep other creatures away. At that point, the rest of its body serves only one purpose —to hide and protect its most vulnerable part.

So what does a strange desert creature have to do with criticism?

In an effort to protect my underbelly, I sometimes get all wrapped up in myself and tragically forget the underbelly of my critic — the place they are vulnerable and the things they might be hiding and protecting beneath the harsh words and prickly exterior. This is a place they may never let me see. It's the storage place for their hurts and disappointments. It holds the root cause of their skepticism and the anger that probably has very little to do with me. Remember, "the mouth speaks what the heart is full of" (Matthew 12:34). And from the overflow of their underbelly, they spewed.

If I forget the other person's underbelly, I am tempted to start storing up my own hurt, skepticism, anger, and disappointments. If I remember this underbelly, I have a much greater chance to keep it all in perspective. I can let my reaction be a good example to this other person just as Luke 21:13 – 15 reminds us: "This will result in you being witnesses to them. But make up your mind not to worry beforehand how you will defend yourselves. For I will give you words and wisdom that none of your adversaries will be able to resist or contradict." Yes, I must make up my mind not to worry about defending myself. Then I uncoil. And I see the opportunity to witness.

Dear Lord, thank You for this challenge to think about the other person's underbelly before I react to criticism. I know it's a simple step, but it's so hard to live out. Help me to put this truth into practice and to walk in the wisdom You have already given. In Jesus' name. Amen.

DAY 38

A Grace Place

Let us then approach God's throne of grace with confidence,
so that we may receive mercy
and find grace to help us in our time of need.

(HEBREWS 4:16)

Thought for the Day:
God is asking me to go to a new place — a place of grace!

I once wondered if God ever got tired of my issues — those recurring failings and sins I couldn't ever seem to conquer. Throughout my lifelong struggle with emotional eating, I whined to God, got mad at God, and often ignored God. And I worried I was going to use up all my grace with God. I felt He would be justified to say, "Enough! Go away. I'm tired of your issues. Figure it out for yourself!"

That is, until I read again the "first story" of God's grace with fresh eyes. We often think of God's grace beginning at the cross. But as I read through the Scripture from the point of view of someone struggling with food issues, I saw a revelation of God's grace right from the start in Genesis.

Adam and Eve disobeyed God by eating from the forbidden tree and ushered sin in to the world. God handed down the consequences of their actions, which included banishment from the Garden of Eden (Genesis 3).

It must have seemed to them that they had pushed past the boundaries of God's grace. After all, He was sending them out of the garden. Whenever I've read that story, I thought they had to leave paradise because God was punishing them. God was disappointed in them. God was giving them what they deserved.

But I was wrong. Their relocation was not a place of abandonment—it was a place of grace.

You see, there were two special trees in the Garden of Eden. One was the tree of the knowledge of good and evil; this was the one with the forbidden fruit. The other was the tree of life. This was the one that gave Adam and Eve perpetual life—no diseases, no death, no sagging body parts. (Okay I'm not sure about that last benefit, but I'm banking on this reality in heaven.)

Anyhow.

When they ate of the tree of the knowledge of good and evil, sin entered in. Sin corrupted everything. And at that point, it was God's absolute love and most tender mercy that ushered Adam and Eve out of the garden. Not His anger or retaliation.

They had to leave. If they'd been allowed to stay, they would have kept eating from the tree of life and lived forever, wallowing in sin. Wallowing in all the brokenness sin brings with it: disease, fear, heartbreak, separation from God. An unending life of shame and sin would have been their fate. And God couldn't stand that for the people He loved.

So, His love made them leave and allowed them to die. So that they could experience the resurrected life His Son would one day provide. Brokenness to redemption.

God did not run out of grace at the dawn of humankind. And He will not run out of grace for you or for me. He does not want us to ever stay in a perpetual state of sin and despair. We were not created with a food struggle or physical cravings because God is angry at us. It is because He loves us so much that He allows our struggle with food to be a physical indication of a spiritual situation. God is asking for us to go to a new place as well—and it is a place of grace!

Receive grace and let it wash away all shame and guilt from every unhealthy choice you've ever regretted and fretted over. Yes, there is work to do and progress to be made, but we will walk from here with a clean slate.

This grace and the unfathomable depth of God's love settle me. Breathes hope into my dread. And trust into my doubts. So when I stumble along on this journey, I know this grace is there for me, and I will come running back. And once again, it will give me a soft place to land.

Dear Lord, thank You for Your grace. Thank You for Your love. Thank You for never giving up on me. Help me to live as Your grateful daughter today. In Jesus' name. Amen.

DAY 39

Weak Places, Strong Places

The LORD is my rock, my fortress and my deliverer;
my God is my rock, in whom I take refuge.

(PSALM 18:2A)

Thought for the Day: Even the smallest drop of God's strength is more than enough to cover our frailties, our shortcomings, the places where we deem ourselves weak.

We all have them. Weak places. Places inside us that make us wonder if we'll ever get it together like the together people. Places that make us feel less than. Less than victorious. Less than a conqueror. Less than strong.

My weak places frustrate me. I just resolved to do better three weeks ago and already I'm slipping in a couple of places. And yet I refuse to resign myself to the thought that I can't ever change.

With the power of Christ, all things can be made new. All broken things are subject to restoration. But sometimes I get so tired of trying and I just feel weak. Can you relate?

What is your weak place? A food issue that rages even though you just signed up for that new diet program? A money situation that seems impossible? A temper that flares? An insecurity that stings?

Let me breathe a little life into your weakness today. Whatever it is, however large it may loom ...

You don't have to have all the answers. You don't have to make suggestions to God. It's okay to be so tired of your weak places that you run out of words to pray.

And listen to the beautiful verses written to us Jesus girls about weak places:

There is now no condemnation for those who are in Christ Jesus. (Romans 8:1)

You, however, are controlled not by the sinful nature but by the Spirit. (Romans 8:9a NIV 1984)

If God is for us, who can be against us? (Romans 8:31b)

No, in all these things we are more than conquerors through him who loved us. (Romans 8:37)

Maybe we need to sit still for just a moment or two today. Quiet, without the weight of condemnation or the swirl of trying to figure things out. Quiet, with nothing but the absolute assurance the Spirit helps us in our weakness.

The Spirit knows what to pray. He understands our weak places. There is a purpose to this weak place. Though it doesn't feel good now, things will be worked out in a way that good will come from it (Romans 8:28).

In that quiet stillness, while the Spirit prays for us and we just simply soak in truth, there will be a flicker of light. A slight trickle of hope. A grace so unimaginable, we'll feel His power overshadowing our weakness. Even the smallest drop of God's strength is more than enough to cover our frailties, our shortcomings, the places where we deem ourselves weak.

And we'll reject that word.

We aren't weak.

We are dependent. Dependent on the only one powerful enough to help us. The only one sufficient enough to cover us in grace throughout the process.

Our relationships may not be sufficient. Our circumstances may not be sufficient. Our finances may not be sufficient. Our willpower may not be sufficient. Our confidence may not be sufficient. But God is and has been and forever will be. He says, "My grace is sufficient for you, for my power is made perfect in weakness" (2 Corinthians 12:9a).

Instead of wallowing in my weak place, I will let the Spirit reveal the one positive step I can take today. I will wash away the condemnation with the warmth of His grace. I will receive His power. And I will rename the weakness my strong place. "For when I am weak, then I am strong" (2 Corinthians 12:10b).

Dear Lord, I am weak without You. Please help me to have enough faith to get through the next challenging situation I will face today. And then enough faith for the next. Thank You for Your love, grace, mercy, and the sacrifice You made on the cross for me. In Jesus' name. Amen.

Pizza Man Grace

Be angry, and yet do not sin;
do not let the sun go down on your anger,
and do not give the devil an opportunity.
(EPHESIANS 4:26–27 NASB)

Thought for the Day:
Accumulated Aggravations = Accumulated Impact

The pizza guy held a delivery bag too small for the requested four larges. I opened the door and smiled. "Four large pizzas, right?"

The look on his face told me the many teens in my backyard were about to be really disappointed. He said, "Ummm, well, actually there's only two. Let me check your ticket ... oh yeah, you're supposed to have four. Give me twenty minutes, and I'll be back with the other two."

I took the two he had and said, "Oh, no problem. The kids can start on these and then have round two when you get back."

As I walked into the kitchen, Art gave me a funny look. "I thought you ordered four pizzas."

"Yeah, the delivery guy forgot two of them but will be back in a few minutes. No big deal," I quipped with a shoulder shrug.

Art tilted his head. "You didn't even ask for a discount or coupons or anything?"

"Oh honey, I felt bad for the guy. It's not a big deal to ask the kids to wait for a few minutes." I smiled.

Thinking of the way I'd reacted during a little "growth opportunity" we'd had earlier, Art said, "Wow. I'd like to get that kind of grace."

Ouch. The point was well made. I'd gotten very aggravated with something Art had done and let him know it. Why is it I'm so quick to give a gentle answer to a stranger but spew on those I love the most?

I think it's because of accumulated impact.

This was the only time I'd ever seen the pizza guy. My emotions toward him were completely neutral. When he made a mistake, I was able to just let it go.

But I have a history with Art. We do lots of life together. If I let little aggravations collect, my emotions ratchet up, creating more and more tension. Then when something happens, I find it much harder to brush it off. Accumulated aggravations ... accumulated impact.

Therefore, it's crucial I don't collect aggravations. I've heard the verse many times: "Do not let the sun go down on your anger" (Ephesians 4:26 NASB). I know it. But honestly, sometimes I ignore it. I go to bed mad anyhow. I collect the aggravations because I'm too tired to talk. Or I don't want to deal with it. Or I try to convince myself it's not a big deal to go to bed mad.

Yet if I keep reading one more verse—Ephesians 4:27—I

understand why I should deal with little aggravations when they are still little. They might not stay little long. Why? Because verse 27 finishes with a strong warning: "Do not give the devil an opportunity."

Yikes.

The devil is just waiting for me to give him an opportunity. I picture him looking at me getting mad over the stupidest things, and hissing, "Go to bed mad ... go to bed mad ... oh yes, go to bed mad and give me an opportunity." That thought sends shivers down my spine.

As well it should.

I love my man. I get aggravated with my man. But I love him. So I certainly don't want to open the door of opportunity for the devil to turn small aggravations into big ones.

So I put down the pizza and kissed my man's cheek. "I love you, and I'm sorry I didn't give you that kind of grace."

To which he replied back with a big smile, "I still think we should have asked for a discount or coupons."

Like I said, I love this man!

Dear Lord, I really want to follow Your example and live a life full of grace. Help me show grace to those closest to me. I don't want to give the devil any opportunities in my marriage, in my relationships with my children, or in my friendships. In Jesus' name. Amen.

DAY 41

The Courageous Choice

Be on your guard; stand firm in the faith;
be courageous; be strong.
(1 CORINTHIANS 16:13)

Thought for the Day: Making a courageous choice means walking on the path of discipline in the area of our food choices. It's coming to the realization that changes need to be made—and making those changes in the quietness of the pantry, when no one else is looking.

I recently had the most interesting conversation with a friend who lives in Hollywood. This person lives in the midst of glitz, glamour, and extreme excess. She lives in that world, but refuses to live like that world. She is determined to teach her kids something rare … the courageous choice. And while Hollywood seems far away from me and my life situations, the courageous choice is something we all face no matter where we live and what issues we're facing.

Throughout this conversation I kept thinking about our courageous choices with food.

You see, there are two kinds of courage. There's the courageous act, which is what makes our heart beat fast when the knight fights the dragon or the firefighter rushes into the burning building. These are extreme events most of us won't ever face. And because most of us aren't put in positions to participate in a courageous act, we don't necessarily think of ourselves as courageous.

But there's a second kind of courage that is widely available but not widely embraced. It's the courageous choice. This is the decision to do the right thing even when it's unpopular, uncelebrated, and probably even unnoticed.

The right thing is to make healthier choices for ourselves. The right thing is to satisfy our deepest needs with God, not food. It's the choice to walk willingly on the path of discipline in the area of our food choices. It's coming to the realization that changes need to be made—and making those changes in the quietness of the pantry, when no one else is looking.

It's respecting ourselves enough to be courageous for us.

It is possible to quiet the battle in your mind. It is possible to make the courageous choice. It is possible to stand in that pantry and declare you were made to consume food but food was never meant to consume you.

It is possible to consume only that which will add to your health and not take away from it. It is possible.

So make that choice. And then make it again. And then make it again.

You are courageous. Now go out and prove it to yourself.

Dear Lord, I acknowledge that I need Your divine help with each choice I make every day. I don't ever want to step outside Your will and direction for my life. I am courageous only with You, in You, and through You. Please help me to embrace Your courageous choices for me. In Jesus' name. Amen.

DAY 42

To-Do List Wisdom

Be gracious in your speech.
The goal is to bring out the best
in others in a conversation,
not put them down, not cut them out.
(COLOSSIANS 4:6 MSG)

Thought for the Day: "When you encounter difficulties and con-
tradictions, do not try to break them, but bend them with gentleness
and time." —FRANCIS DE SALES

Some of us write out our to-do lists each day. Others of us are more
creative (less organized), and we keep our lists floating around in
our brains or just fly by the seat of our pants.

Either way, all of us have things we need to get done each day.

Recently my thirteen-year-old daughter, Brooke, tweeted her
to-do list.

And, y'all, the preciousness of her list made my heart dance
with joy. And it challenged me.

She's a relationship-driven gal. I'm a task-oriented gal. Neither is
better. However, I'm challenged when I look at Brooke's list and see

that she puts as much intentionality into building her relationships each day as she does into accomplishing her tasks.

Are you ready to see the cutest, sweetest to-do list ever written?

1. Bring project for [social studies] on Ashley's laptop

2. Take allergy meds

3. Tell Mom u love her

4. Text Kenzi to tell her if u are going to school

5. Thank Jesus for being there for u

6. Give Daddy a hug

7. Eat breakfast

8. Take shower (hair looks bad)

9. Tell Ashley she is the best big sister

10. Tell Hope she looks really pretty

My to-do lists don't look like this. They are filled with tasks and errands, which aren't bad, but I do need to get more intentional with relationship building, so maybe adding more relationship-oriented items to my list might help me.

Are you more task-oriented or relationship-oriented? What to-do items do you need to get more intentional about—tasks or relationship building?

Maybe, just maybe, we can use Brooke's sweet to-do list to help formulate our Gentle Reply List.

- How can you honor someone who feels offended today?

- How can you show grace to "your people" today?

- How can you show compassion to that hard-to-love person today?

Yesterday we talked about accepting the challenge to hold our tongues and offer a gentle reply instead of spewing. Today, let's ask the Lord to show us how to love those around us, tempering our responses with honor, grace, and compassion.

Dear Lord, thank You for the people You have placed in my life. Even the ones who are sometimes difficult. I want to honor them by showing grace and compassion today. Help me be intentional with my actions and responses. In Jesus' name. Amen.

DAY 43

A Soul Longing to Be Filled

I spread out my hands to you;
I thirst for you like a parched land.

(PSALM 143:6)

Thought for the Day: When the desire for treats is triggered by difficult emotions, it's not really a desire for treats. It's a thinly veiled attempt at self-medication.

A starved soul is like the vacuum cleaner my mother used when I was a child. It had a long metal tube that ravenously sucked up anything and everything set before it. It sucked up dust bunnies with the same furor as a $10 bill. I know that one from experience.

Our souls have the same ravenous intensity as my mother's vacuum cleaner; that's how God created us—with a longing to be filled. It's a longing God instilled to draw us into deep intimacy with Him. The psalmist expresses this longing as an intense thirst:

As the deer pants for streams of water, so my soul pants for you, my God. My soul thirsts for God, for the living God. When can I go and meet with God? (Psalm 42:1–2)

I spread out my hands to you; I thirst for you like a parched land. (Psalm 143:6)

Indeed, our souls are thirsty and ravenous vacuums. If we fail to understand how to fill our souls with spiritual nourishment, we will forever be triggered to numb our longings with other temporary physical pleasures. When those pleasures are food, the resulting behavior is what we often hear referred to as "emotional eating." But this issue is bigger than emotions; it's really about spiritual deprivation.

My boyfriend breaks up with me. I want a tub of ice cream.

That big business deal falls through. I'll take the super-sized fries, please.

I don't feel pretty. I need some chocolate to soothe and delight me.

My kids are driving me crazy. I deserve a piece of cake. I deserve three pieces.

I hate cleaning my house. When I'm done I'll treat myself to as many chips as I want.

It's my birthday and I don't really think anyone cares. I'll just eat my way into happiness or numbness.

Same difference, right?

I hardly think it ironic that I'm struggling even as I write these words. There's a situation in my life that has wormed its way straight to the most vulnerable of places in my heart. This situation has made me feel hurt and rejected. Years ago a little crack in my strong resolve was created by the extreme rejection of my biological father. And while I've found amazing victory in understanding I'm no longer a child of a broken parent but rather a child of God, revisiting rejection is never fun.

I'm not saying we shouldn't allow ourselves the occasional treat. We should. But I've realized when the desire for treats is triggered by difficult emotions, it's not really a desire for treats. It's a thinly veiled attempt at self-medication. And self-medicating with food even once triggers vicious cycles I must avoid.

When difficult emotions come, I must realize stuffing myself with food only serves to compound the bad feelings later. What I need in this moment is to do something good, positive, and healthy for myself. Take a walk, read an inspirational book, write an encouraging note to a friend, memorize an uplifting verse, or play some of my favorite praise songs really loudly while driving through the country. This is just a start of my list of positive things to do that refresh me. What would be on your list? What refreshes, refuels, and refills your soul?

> *Dear Lord, I have connected emotional emptiness with a desire*
> *for more food. Please help me to deal with these triggers so*
> *I can recognize them for what they are and put them to rest.*
> *In Jesus' name. Amen.*

DAY 44

You Don't Like Me

And the peace of God, which transcends all understanding,
will guard your hearts and your minds in Christ Jesus.
(PHILIPPIANS 4:7)

Thought for the Day: Toxic thoughts leave no room for truth to flourish. And in the absence of truth, lies reign.

Have you ever had thoughts of insecurity so strangling you thought you might choke? Thoughts like ...

You are not liked.

Who are you to think you could do that?

Why did you say that? Everyone thinks you're annoying.

Your kids just illustrated every inadequacy you have as a mom.

You are invisible.

If you've never had words like these run rampant through your thoughts, lift your hands up in sheer praise.

For the rest of us, let's go there today. Because, honestly, we unglued girls need to go there. To the inner places of secret thoughts and harsh self-condemnations. If there were one gift I wish I could give every woman on the planet, it would be the ability to silence the destructive words we allow to fall hard on our souls. Toxic thoughts leave no room for truth to flourish. And in the absence of truth, lies reign.

The other day I was discussing something with my husband, and I said, "I know you think I'm being annoying and overly protective about this but ..."

Art stopped me and said, "How do you know that's what I'm thinking? Please don't hold me liable for saying things that are really only thoughts in your mind."

Sheer brilliance.

He's so right. *He* hadn't said those things. I was assuming he was thinking them and operating as if those toxic thoughts were reality.

I think we girls do this way too often. People aren't thinking about us and assessing us nearly as much as we think they are. Honestly, they don't have time. Because they are probably spending too much time thinking about and assessing themselves. Do you see the crazy in all this?

I do.

That's why we've got to hold our thoughts to a higher standard. How dare they be allowed to simply parade about as if they are true and manipulate us into feeling insecure, inadequate, and misunderstood! Oh, how much trouble we invite into our lives when our thoughts are based on assumptions.

So here are three questions we'd do well to ask ourselves when thoughts are dragging us down.

1. *Did someone actually say this or am I making assumptions about what they're thinking?*

If they actually said it, then I need to deal with it. If I'm assuming it, that's unfair to them and damaging to me. Philippians 4:6 invites me to choose prayer over worry in every situation. Instead of allowing my thoughts to overtake me, whether in assumptions or despair, I can ask God to shine His truth into my situation. "Do not be anxious about anything, but in everything by prayer and supplication with thanksgiving let your requests be made known to God" (NASB).

2. *Am I actively immersing myself in truth?*

The more I read God's truths and let truth fill my mind, the less time I'll spend contemplating untruths. Philippians 4:7 holds a promise for me when I turn to God and allow His truth to fill me: my heart is protected by peace. "And the peace of God, which surpasses all comprehension, will guard your hearts and your minds in Christ Jesus" (NASB).

3. *Are there situations or relationships that feed my insecurities?*

If so, maybe I need to take a break from these for a season. "Finally, brothers and sisters, whatever is true, whatever is noble, whatever is right, whatever is pure, whatever is lovely, whatever is admirable—if anything is excellent or praiseworthy—think about such things" (Philippians 4:8).

Good gracious, I know this is tough stuff. I know these issues can be more complicated than three simple questions. But it's a good place to start holding our thoughts accountable.

After all, how a woman thinks is often how she lives.

I think we need to read that one again, don't you? *How a woman thinks is often how she lives.* May we think on and live out truth —and only truth—today.

> *Dear Lord, fix my heart and mind on You today so that I will experience Your peace. Help me recognize and control unhealthy thoughts. In Jesus' name. Amen.*

Pretending I'm Fine, Proving I'm Right

*But the wisdom that comes from heaven is first of all pure;
then peace-loving, considerate, submissive,
full of mercy and good fruit, impartial and sincere.*

(JAMES 3:17)

Thought for the Day: If I catch myself pretending or proving, I know I'm processing my hurt the wrong way.

If someone says something or does something that hurts me, what is the godly response? Is it to pretend that everything is fine so I can keep the peace? Or is it to confront the person to prove how wrong she is?

Neither.

If ever I catch myself pretending or proving, I know I'm processing my hurt the wrong way.

The right way is approaching this situation with soul integrity —responding in a way that's not only honest but peacemaking. James 3:17 says, "But the wisdom that comes from heaven is first of all pure [honest]; then peace-loving ..." Yes, I want this kind of wisdom, this soul integrity. I want to be honest and peacemaking at the same time. But how?

Real honesty. Not all honest expressions of my feelings are real honesty. You see, my honest feelings may not be truthful assessments of the situation. I can be honest with how I feel and still exaggerate or misinterpret what is true. I can feel justified in being blatant about my feelings—not hiding a thing—and prideful for being so real, all under the guise of being honest enough not to stuff.

But in reality, honesty that isn't true isn't honesty at all. It may just be emotional spewing. That's why we need peacemaking honesty—honesty reined in by the Holy Spirit—if we're going to have authentic soul integrity.

So if I want real honesty, I have to ask the Holy Spirit to show me real truth. I need to see things from the other person's perspective. I need to ask questions of that person with the desire to better understand instead of throwing out statements of accusation. Ultimately, my goal should be to add peacemaking to my honesty.

Real peacemaking. At the same time, it must also grieve God to see plastic versions of peacemaking that aren't reined in by honesty. That's what we do when we stuff and pretend everything is okay. The upside of stuffing is that we have the semblance of peacemakers. But when we do so at the expense of honesty, we harbor a corrosive bitterness that will eventually emerge. Either it will erode our health and later present itself in a host of emotional and physical anxiety-induced illnesses, or it will accumulate over time and surprise everyone when the peacemaker eventually erupts. Saying "I'm fine" to keep the peace, when we're really not fine, isn't honest.

Sometimes dishonesty comes in the form of saying things that aren't true. But it's also dishonest when we fail to say things that are true.

It may seem godly in the moment, but it's false godliness. Truth and godliness always walk hand in hand. The minute we divorce one from the other, we stray from soul integrity and give a foothold to the instability that inevitably leads to coming unglued.

Yes, we're after soul integrity — honesty that is also peacemaking that leads to godliness. This soul integrity brings balance to unglued reactions. It makes us true peacemakers — people who aren't proving or pretending but rather honestly demonstrating what they are experiencing in a godly manner. And being a true peacemaker reaps a harvest of great qualities in our lives: right things, godly things, healthy things.

Dear Lord, through You I am able to bring all my exploding and stuffing under Your authority and truth. Thank You for Your Holy Spirit who gives me the wisdom to move beyond my reactions. Help me lean on You. In Jesus' name. Amen.

DAY 46

A Supernatural Fix

Come to me,
all you who are weary and burdened,
and I will give you rest.
(MATTHEW 11:28)

Thought for the Day: I can only find rest—fresh hope—as I stop resisting God's truths and start applying them.

Honestly, I'm tired of this being my issue! Why doesn't God step in and just supernaturally fix this?

Have you ever felt this way?

God understands what it's like to feel worn out and tired of struggling, and He hears our cry. Jesus encourages us, "Come to me, all you who are weary and burdened, and I will give you rest" (Matthew 11:28).

I used to get so frustrated when I heard this verse because I thought, "I don't want rest—I want to be restored! I want to be rid of this weight struggle once and for all!"

But the gift of rest Jesus is offering here is not a spiritual Ambien. The Greek word for this kind of rest is *anapauo* (an-ap-ow´-o) which means "of calm and patient expectation." In other words, Jesus is saying, "If you come to me, I will take your exhaustion in this area and turn it into expectation. In this place you feel hopeless, I can make you hopeful."

But how?

My friend Jennifer Rothschild does this enlightening exercise at some of her conferences. She tells the audience to imagine her writing two different words on a large chalkboard. She then speaks the letters as she draws the first word into the air ... R-E-S-T. She does the same for the second word ... R-E-S-I-S-T. Then she asks, "What's the difference?"

The difference is, of course, "I."

I can't do this. *I* can't say no. *I* can't make lasting changes. *I* don't see how the Bible can really help with this struggle.

I'm familiar with these "I" statements because I've said them myself.

We can only find *anapauo* rest—fresh hope—as we stop resisting God's truths and start applying them. Quickly skim back over the truths we've already covered in this book and find one you highlighted, got all inspired by, but haven't yet applied. Write it on a 3 x 5 card and then keep reading.

One of the assignments Jesus gives us is to take on His yoke and learn from Him (Matthew 11:29). In other words, discipline and work are necessary.

This is your part of the equation.

But after the assignment comes reassurance, "My yoke is easy and my burden is light" (Matthew 11:30). God knows where your strength ends and that is the exact point where His strength begins.

This is God's part of the equation.

I must do all I can do. Then God will do what only He can do.

My pastor, Steven Furtick, says, "You bring the natural. God will then bring the super. And that's what creates supernatural."

Dear Lord, I want to wait in calm and patient expectation today. Please take my exhaustion and turn it into expectation; take my feelings of hopelessness and give me real hope. I want to stop resisting Your truths and start applying them. I will do all that I can today, and I will wait with anticipation for all that You will do through me. In Jesus' name. Amen.

DAY 47

Disappointment

Take delight in the LORD,
and he will give you the desires of your heart.
(PSALM 37:4)

Thought for the Day:
Disappointment only stings as long as I let it.

The other day a friend asked me if I ever get disappointed. I said yes and threw out a spiritually sound answer. And then the next day happened. The day when a really big disappointment whacked me upside the head and sent my heart sinking. I'd been asked to speak at a really big event — one of the biggest of my life — and then things fell apart.

Invited, thrilled, excited, honored, included turned into uninvited, bummed, sad, disillusioned, left out. And while I still had solid spiritual perspectives to hold on to, my flesh just needed a minute to say, "Stink!"

Because sometimes things do stink. But right when I wanted say "Stink" a few more times, I spotted a bowl that's been sitting on my dining room table for weeks now. Brooke found some caterpillars awhile back, put them in a bowl, and has been holding them hostage ever since. I mean she's been lovingly admiring them underneath a layer of cellophane.

Wouldn't you know that those caterpillars formed cocoons inside that unlikely environment. And then today, as I was muttering, "Stink!" I glanced across that bowl and sucked the word back down my throat.

The cocoons were empty.

Expecting glorious butterflies, I had to chuckle when I got right over the bowl and closely examined the product of my little girl's hopes for new life.

Moths.

Yet another thing in my day that wasn't quite right.

Or was it?

When Brooke spotted the moths, she was beyond thrilled. Grabbing my hand, she led me outside, ripped off the plastic barrier, and watched the beauty of tiny wings beating ... beating ... beating ... and finally fluttering into flight.

Hmmmm.

As I watched Brooke's sheer delight, I realized she couldn't have cared less if they were moths or butterflies. Creatures that once knew only the dirt of the earth had just been given the gift of flight. Reaching, soaring up, up, and away.

And with that realization, this simple creature pulled up the corners of her mouth into a smile.

Disappointment only stings as long as I let it.

Dear Lord, thank You for Your mercies and patience in this journey of imperfect progress. Forgive me for allowing disappointment to capture my heart so easily. Adjust my perspective and help me to see the things You have brought to life in me. In Jesus' name. Amen.

DAY 48

I Need _____!

And my God will meet all your needs
according to the riches of his glory in Christ Jesus.
(PHILIPPIANS 4:19)

Thought for the Day:
Temptation is an invitation to meet my needs
outside the will of God.

Satan's very name means "one who casts something between two to cause a separation." He wants to separate us from God. One of the subtle ways he does this is to raise doubts in our mind about whether or not God will meet our needs, if God is truly enough. Satan wants us to feel alone and abandoned so that we turn to his offerings instead.

Temptation of any kind is Satan's invitation to meet our needs outside the will of God—through material things, chasing significance and approval from others, or excessive physical desires.

Often the script that plays in our head is, "I need _____ so I can be satisfied."

It's what causes a woman on a budget to set off on a spending spree. She feels the thrill of the purchase in the moment. But shame creeps in as she hides the telltale shopping bags from her family.

It's what pulls at the businesswoman to work harder and longer and refuse to build boundaries in her schedule. Always chasing that next accomplishment or that next compliment—but it's never enough.

It's what sent me on many eating sprees. The kids were loud; the house was messy; the demands of life felt beyond my control. So with great justification, I'd indulge only to end up with a bloated stomach and a deflated heart.

We expose this subtle message sold to us by Satan when we break it down to distinguish the difference between a need and a want.

All of the examples I just described are *wants*, not *needs*. Intellectually, we understand the definition of each of these words, but oh how Satan wants us to think they are one and the same.

When the difference between these two words starts to blur, we are on the road to compromising. We start justifying. And it sets us up to meet our needs outside the will of God. The abyss of discontentment invites us in and threatens to darken and distort everything in our world.

Remember, Satan is a liar. The more we fill ourselves with his distorted desires, the emptier we'll feel. The more we overspend, overwork, or overeat, the emptier we feel. Satan wants to separate you from God's best plans. He wants to separate you from God's proper provision. He wants to separate you from God's peace.

God's provision sustains life. Satan's temptation drains life.

God's provision in the short term will reap blessings in the long term. Satan's temptation in the short term will reap heartache in the long term.

God's provision satisfies the soul. Satan's temptation gratifies the flesh.

Oh sweet sister, consider these realities when making choices today. The apostle Paul writes, "My God will meet all your needs according to the riches of his glory in Christ Jesus" (Philippians 4:19). That's a promise. Trust God. Embrace truth. Live His promise.

Dear Lord, I am reminded once again of how dangerous temptations are, because they invite me to meet my needs outside of Your will. Keep me from compromising and from justifying today. I know that only Your provision sustains life and satisfies my soul. I want this truth to ring loud and clear throughout my day today. In Jesus' name. Amen.

Turning North

You have circled this mountain long enough.
Now turn north.
(DEUTERONOMY 2:3 NASB)

Thought for the Day:
Am I letting this mess *define* me or *refine* me?

We all have messes in our lives. We've been talking about the mess we can get into when we let our eating issues get out of control. But we face other types of messes as well. Financial messes. Relationship messes. Health messes. Kid messes. Home messes. Business messes.

Sometimes our messes are small and feel only like a slight annoyance. Other times, they're so huge they strip the hope right out of our lives. But here's a thought to ponder right in the midst of your mess . . .

Am I letting this mess *define* me or *refine* me?

The answer to this question is crucial.

If I am letting a mess *define* me, I will feel *hopeless*.

If I am letting a mess *refine* me, I will be *hopeful*.

It's time for our messes to stop defining us.

It's time to embrace the refining process and "turn north."

If you find yourself stuck in a mess, try replacing your old self-defeating thoughts with empowering new thoughts. I call these "go-to scripts," statements of biblical truth that allow the Messiah to touch our mess and turn it into a great message of hope. Consider these:

1. *I was made for more than to be stuck in a vicious cycle of defeat.*

   "You have circled this mountain long enough. Now turn north" (Deuteronomy 2:3 NASB).

2. *When I am considering a compromise, I will think past this moment and ask myself, how will I feel about this choice tomorrow morning?*

   "Do you not know that your bodies are temples of the Holy Spirit, who is in you, whom you have received from God? You are not your own; you were bought at a price. Therefore honor God with your bodies" (1 Corinthians 6:19–20).

3. *When tempted, I will either remove the temptation or remove myself from the situation.*

   "God is faithful; he will not let you be tempted beyond what you can bear. But when you are tempted, he will also provide a way out so that you can endure it. Therefore, my dear friends, flee ..." (1 Corinthians 10:13b–14a).

4. *I don't have to worry about letting God down because I was never holding Him up; God's grace is sufficient.*

"But he said to me, 'My grace is sufficient for you, for my power is made perfect in weakness.'... For when I am weak, then I am strong'" (2 Corinthians 12:9–10).

5. *I have these boundaries in place not for restriction but rather to define the parameters of my freedom.*

"I put this in human terms because you are weak in your natural selves. Just as you used to offer the parts of your body in slavery to impurity and to ever-increasing wickedness, so now offer them in slavery to righteousness leading to holiness" (Romans 6:19 NIV 1984).

I keep these go-to scripts on the top of my mind so they interrupt the excuses I had become accustomed to believing for too long. Let some version of these statements bump into your reality and redefine your old patterns of thought. It will change the way you think!

And when we change the way we think, we'll be better equipped to change the way we make choices.

Dear Lord, help me to embrace and apply the truth in these go-to scripts. When I am weak, then I am strong. I want to leave my old eating habits behind me and turn this corner for good. In Jesus' name. Amen.

DAY 50

The Best Worst Thing

And we know that in all things God works
for the good of those who love him.
(ROMANS 8:28)

Thought for the Day: God can take our worst and add His best.
We just have to make the choice to stay with Him and keep following
Him through it all.

I failed at being a wedding planner. No one wants a planner who
gets so undone by the neurotic mother of the bride that she throws
up in the parking lot right beside the guest sidewalk. Really, nothing says, "Welcome to my wedding," quite like that.

I failed at being a kitchen gadget saleswoman. No one wants to
see the tip of a thumb sliced off into the veggie pizza at the exact
moment I was promising how safe this gadget is. Awesome.

I failed at being a cafeteria lady at a private school. My assistant
decided her arms were so dry she needed to coat herself with our
spray butter. When we took the trash out later that day, we both got
attacked by bees and forgot about the pizza in the oven. Kids don't
take kindly to burnt pizza.

I failed at being a receptionist. It's never a good idea to just succumb to those sleepy afternoon feelings and lay your head down on the desk. Bosses don't like workers who snore. Even if they are pregnant.

Yes, I failed at a lot during those years when I was trying to figure out what to do with my life. At the time, each of these things felt like the worst thing that could have happened. Now I think they were the *best worst things*.

Had I been successful at these things, I never would have discovered the joy of being in the ministry I'm in now. I see this same theme woven throughout many stories in the Bible.

Jesus is getting into a boat with His disciples. "Without warning, a furious storm came up on the lake, so that the waves swept over the boat" (Matthew 8:23 – 24). Worst thing. But then Jesus gets up and rebukes the winds and waves, and things turn completely calm. The disciples are amazed. *Best worst thing.*

The apostles are being arrested and thrown in jail (Acts 5:12). Worst thing. But then an angel of the Lord opens the doors of the jail and brings them out. Later, they are so full of confidence they boldly proclaim, "We must obey God rather than human beings!" (Acts 5:29). *Best worst thing.*

Jesus is crucified and dies on a cross. Worst thing. But then on the third day he rises from the grave, making a way for us to be forgiven from our sins. *Best worst thing.*

I don't understand why we have to go through cruddy stuff. And I certainly know there are far worse things to go through than a few job changes.

We live in a broken world full of broken people. But isn't it comforting to know God is never broken? He isn't ever caught off guard, taken by surprise, or shocked by what happens next.

He can take our worst and add His best. We just have to make the choice to stay with Him and keep following Him through it all.

Even a neurotic mother of the bride who makes a wedding planner's stomach work in reverse can become a *best worst thing.*

Dear Lord, I can't begin to say how grateful I am that You turn all things for good. All things. Give me faith to believe and see. Thanks so much. In Jesus' name. Amen.

DAY 51

What Frustrated Jesus

I will remember the deeds of the LORD;
yes, I will remember your miracles of long ago.
(PSALM 77:11)

Thought for the Day:
I can be the unglued woman
made gentle, patient, and peaceful.

If I lived in Jesus' day, I would like to think I'd have been moved by His miracles. Changed by His miracles. Repentant and willing to live differently because of His miracles. He is the Son of God —the miracle worker.

But would I really?

After all, sometimes I act as though Jesus can work miracles for other people, but not for me. Not with my issues.

Last year, my issues with coming unglued and getting all tangled in my raw emotions constantly left me making promises to do better tomorrow. But then tomorrow would bring with it more challenges and conflicts where I'd react and then regret. No, I wasn't sure Jesus could work a miracle with my issues. I was quick to applaud when other people repented and positioned their hearts to see Jesus work a miracle in their lives, but I lived as if that same kind of miracle wasn't possible for me.

This kind of unrepentant attitude frustrates Jesus. Matthew says that Jesus "began to denounce the towns in which most of his miracles had been performed, because they did not repent" (11:20).

Sometimes I have to get out of my normal surroundings to become more aware of things that need to change in me. Last year I spent a week at a homeless shelter called the Dream Center in Los Angeles. Pastor Matthew Barnett and his church run the Dream Center, which is a ministry hub of 120 programs that serve more than 40,000 people every month. Housed in a converted hospital building, the 700-bed facility includes a transitional shelter for homeless families, a drug rehab center, and a shelter for victims of sex trafficking.

I went to help meet needs. But I quickly realized I was there as a woman in need. A woman who needed God's reality to fall fresh and heavy and close and real and too in-my-face to deny.

I saw God's miraculous healing power woven into so many lives at the Dream Center. I saw it, and I wanted it.

God's miraculous power is what transformed the ex–gang member with eight bullet hole scars into a Jesus-loving servant. So gentle.

It's what changed the ex–prostitute into a counselor for other girls rescued from life on the streets. So pure.

It's what changed the ex–drug addict into a loving father, teaching his son how to be a godly leader. So integrity-filled.

What prevented me from realizing that God's power could change me too? Somewhere along the line I stopped expecting God to work miraculously in me.

Inspired by the changed lives at the homeless shelter, my soul quickened to the bold reality that I could be different. I really could have different reactions to my raw emotions. I knew my progress would be imperfect, but it could still be miraculous. And I felt a new hope rush through me.

I'm not gentle by nature, but I can be gentle by obedience. I'm not patient by nature, but I can be patient by obedience. I'm not peaceful by nature, but I can be peaceful by obedience.

I can. And I will.

I can be the unglued woman made gentle, patient, and peaceful. God, help me. God, forgive me. And in the shadow of that realization and repentance, the miracle begins.

Dear Lord, please open my eyes to see the places I need You to change in me. I know I have wrapped my identity in so many things other than You. I want You to change those rough, imperfect places in my heart. Help me become the woman You created me to be. In Jesus' name. Amen.

DAY 52

The Cost

... in order that Satan might not outwit us.
For we are not unaware of his schemes.
(2 CORINTHIANS 2:11)

Thought for the Day:
How much will this really cost me?

It is so crucial that we understand the fight we are in for our health, our families, our attitudes, our marriages, our friendships, our journey toward freedom. Satan wants not just to discourage us but to destroy us. His attacks are not just willy-nilly attempts to trip us up or knock us down. He wants to take us out.

I have a fire in my belly about how crafty and strategic Satan really is. He has made me fighting mad recently, and I can't help but address it.

Do you know why Satan's tactics are called schemes (2 Corinthians 2:10–11)? A scheme is a plan, design, or program of action. Satan's tactics are called schemes because they are well thought through plans specifically targeted to do three things:

1. To increase your desire for something outside the will of God.
2. To make you think giving in to a weakness is no big deal.
3. To minimize your ability to think through the consequences of falling to this temptation.

Oh how I wish we could see the cost of each of our choices as clearly as a price tag on store merchandise. Or as clearly as the caloric cost of food choices offered on menus in New York. (Did you know restaurants in New York are required to put nutritional information on their menus? Fabulous!) If I know how much something is going to cost me, I make much wiser choices.

Satan is a master of keeping that cost hidden until it's too late.

Here's how pastor and author Chip Ingram characterizes Satan's schemes:

> They are orchestrated in order to tempt us, deceive us, draw us away from God, fill our hearts with half-truths and untruths, and lure us into pursuing good things in the wrong way, at the wrong time, or with the wrong person. The English word *strategies* is derived from the Greek word Paul uses that is translated "schemes." That means our temptations are not random. The false perspectives we encounter do not come at us haphazardly. The lies we hear, the conflicts we have with others, the cravings that consume us when we are at our weakest points — they are all part of a plan to make us casualties in the invisible war. They are organized, below-the-belt assaults designed to neutralize the very people God has filled with his awesome power.[*]

Sweet sisters, I think this is something worth thinking about.

---

[*]Chip Ingram, *The Invisible War* (Grand Rapids: Baker, 2006), 27.

How much will this really cost me? If we do nothing else this week but consistently apply this one question to every choice, we will have invested wisely. So, so very wisely.

Dear Lord, please help me to focus on You today and the perfect plan You have for my life. I am reminded that boldly following You is so much better than any short-term experience that is not pleasing to You. Give me Your eyes so that I can see temptation and its many different faces. In Jesus' name. Amen.

DAY 53

Why Am I Scared
to Pray Boldly?

*The prayer of a righteous person
is powerful and effective.*
(JAMES 5:16B)

Thought for the Day: Prayer does make a difference — a life-changing, mind-blowing, earth-rattling difference. We don't need to know how. We don't need to know when. We just need to kneel confidently and know the tremors of a simple Jesus girl's prayers extend far wide and far high and far deep.

Have you ever caught yourself in this journey toward health being a little reserved in prayer? Me too. Especially when it comes to bold commitment prayers.

Prayers where I boldly commit this journey to God. Prayers where I commit to following through. Prayers where I declare the Scriptures we've been studying as promises I can live out. Prayers where I ask God to help hold me accountable.

It's not at all that I don't believe God can do anything. I absolutely do. I'm a wild-about-Jesus girl. Wild in my willingness. Wild in my obedience. Wild in my adventures with God.

My hesitation isn't rooted in any kind of doubt about God. It's more rooted in doubts about myself and a hyper awareness of my weaknesses.

Can you relate?

I so desperately want to stay in the absolute will of God that I sometimes find myself praying with clauses. Like, "God, I want to commit this journey to You, but I'm really scared I'm going to fail." I wonder why I don't just boldly pray, "God, I commit this journey to You. The whole thing. The times I'm successful and the times I need grace." And then stand confidently that my prayers were not in vain no matter what the outcome.

The reality is God wants me to boldly pray. I am convinced boldly praying changes me. It boots me out of that stale place of religious habit into authentic connection with God Himself.

Prayer opens my spiritual eyes to see things I can't see on my own. And I am convinced prayer changes circumstances. Prayers are powerful and effective if prayed from the position of a righteous heart (James 5:16).

Prayer does make a difference — a life-changing, mind-blowing, earth-rattling difference. We don't need to know how. We don't need to know when. We just need to kneel confidently and know the tremors of a simple Jesus girl's prayers extend far wide and far high and far deep.

Letting that absolute truth slosh over into my soul snuffs out the flickers of hesitation. It bends my stiff knees. And it ignites a fresh, bold, even wilder fire within me. Not bold as in bossy and demanding. But bold as in, *I love my Jesus with all my heart, so why would I offer anything less than an ignited prayer life?*

So let's ask God boldly for what we need in all aspects of our lives. Including this Made to Crave journey. Maybe especially for this ongoing Made to Crave journey. And then ask again. Not so that we can manipulate the movement of God. But rather so we can position our souls to really follow Jesus throughout this entire journey.

And with that, our devotions come to an end. But I can't think of a better place to leave you than tucked safely in the arms of a Jesus to whom we absolutely must boldly pray.

Dear Lord, I believe that You are the giver of life and Lord over all things. Help me to pray with a fresh new boldness today. I am convinced that prayers change me. I trust You and depend on You, Lord, and seek to follow You in every way. In Jesus' name. Amen.

DAY 54

Is My Pain Talking?

We take captive every thought
to make it obedient to Christ.
(2 CORINTHIANS 10:5)

Thought for the Day:
Our Lord doesn't whisper shameful condemnations.

Have you ever been in a situation where something little felt really big? Maybe a look from someone that suddenly makes you feel they don't like you at all. Or when someone doesn't return your phone call and you feel like it's an indication that you're not important.

Usually these things aren't true. The look was just a look with no hidden meaning. The missed phone call was just a slip on that person's to-do list. But if we're not careful, those misguided feelings can create issues that distract us, discourage us, and trigger past pain to start taunting us.

It happened to me on a certain Friday. My sister, Angee, and I got up at 3:00 a.m. and were in line at a certain retail establishment thirty minutes later. I know. I agree. That's crazy. But like a hunter stalking prey, I was after something. In this case, the buy-one-get-one-free washer and dryer. Angee was after a half-priced computer. When the store doors opened at 5:00 a.m., we both scored. Happiness abounded. Then we left to get some breakfast. This is the part of the story where the happiness faded.

In the drive-thru, my credit card was "not approved."

Let me get this straight. It *was* approved at the store just five minutes ago when I made a major purchase. But now for a little two-dollar bundle of egg, cheese, Canadian bacon, and English muffin, suddenly I'm *not* approved?

Not approved.

Not approved.

Ouch.

My sister wasn't fazed a bit. She whipped out cash, paid for my breakfast, and headed to the next store on our list. But those words "not approved" hung like a black cloud over my head. It bothered the stink out of me. I knew it was just some technical glitch, but that's not what it felt like.

When that girl leaned out of the drive-thru window and in a hushed tone said, "I'm sorry, ma'am, but your card keeps coming up as not approved," it felt personal. Really personal.

Suddenly, my past pain and current embarrassment started running its mouth inside my head. *You're nothing but a loser. You are unwanted. You are unloved. You are so disorganized. You are poor. You are not acceptable. You are not approved.* And all that pent-up yuck came spewing out on my kids later that afternoon.

I wish I could tie up this story in a nice bow and give you a pretty ending, but I can't. It was anything but pretty. I felt awful. And I went to bed wondering if the Lord Himself might come down and say, "Lysa TerKeurst, I have had enough of your immature reactions. You are no longer approved to be a Bible study teacher. Look at you!"

But that's not the Lord's voice. Our Lord doesn't whisper shameful condemnations. Convictions, yes. Condemnations, no.

As I stared wide-eyed into the darkness that enveloped the room, I whispered, "Give me Your voice, Jesus. I need to hear You above all this mess. If I don't hear You, I'm afraid this darkness is going to swallow me alive." Nothing came. I couldn't hear a thing.

So I had a choice. I could lie there in the dark replaying the awful events of the day, or I could turn the light on and read God's Word —His truth—which is the best thing to do when lies are swarming and attacking like a bunch of bloodthirsty mosquitoes. Lies flee in the presence of truth. And while reading God's truth that night didn't change the fact that I needed to make things right with my kids the next day, it sure did give me the courage to do so.

Dear Lord, please drown out the other voices ... please hush them ... and speak. I want to hear You above all the noise. In Jesus' name. Amen.

DAY 55

The Stuffer Who
Builds Barriers

*And God is able to make all grace abound to you,
so that having all sufficiency in all things at all times,
you may abound in every good work.*
(2 CORINTHIANS 9:8 ESV)

Thought for the Day: It's unfair of me to use my expectations as the standard for someone else's behavior or hold it against her when she doesn't live up to my hopes.

What often opens the door of conflict in my relationships is expectations. There are two kinds of expectations: realistic and unrealistic. Unrealistic expectations are things another person isn't able or willing to do for me. I have to let go of these. Certainly God can either change that person or change me by rearranging my desires. In the meantime, it's unfair of me to use my expectations as the standard for other people's behavior or hold it against them when they don't live up to my hopes.

Realistic expectations, on the other hand, are things I *can* reasonably expect another person to do for me. Of course, it's important to discern how to communicate these expectations with gentleness and at the right time. Timing is key.

My pastor's wife, Holly Furtick, recently told me how she discerns the timing of such conversations with her husband, Steven. She prays specifically that God will make it clear to her when the time is right to have non-emotionally charged conversations of gentle confrontation or clarification. As she's running errands, fixing dinner, or flipping through her fashion magazines (the girl loves fashion!), she prays for God to make the timing clear. And He does!

She'd been wanting to talk to Steven about something that had been bothering her, but she didn't want it to become a big deal. She determined it was a realistic expectation on her part, so she committed to pray for the right timing. A few weeks later, she and Steven were coming home from a trip. They'd had a great time. Suddenly, he slid a piece of paper her way and said, "Write down three things I could do better as your husband."

Holly smiled. This was exactly what she'd been praying for —but even better! Her husband was the one who paved the way for a healthy conversation. God doesn't always work so quickly in answering our timing prayers, but what a comfort and encouragement to see how God paved the way for a "clarifying expectations" conversation.

Why not take your expectations and your need for discernment about them to God in prayer? Why not ask Him to get involved? Holly's example inspired me and has given me yet another tool to keep me from stuffing and building barriers. Again, I won't minimize how hard these things can be. But imperfect progress is possible and gets us unstuck from unrealistic expectations that can so easily lead to barrier building in our relationships.

Dear Lord, thank You for going before me in every difficult situation. I want to pause and wait on Your leading before I speak. But I do want to speak instead of stuffing and building barriers. Teach me to seek You and know the right way to communicate in my situation. In Jesus' name. Amen.

DAY 56

Finish the Work

I tell you, open your eyes and look at the fields!
They are ripe for harvest.
(JOHN 4:35B)

Thought for the Day:
Food can fill my stomach but never my soul.

If you've attended many Christian women's events, you've probably heard the story of the Samaritan woman told from just about every possible angle. If I hear someone start to speak about her at a conference, I'll admit my brain begs me to tune out and daydream about tropical places or items I need to add to my grocery list.

It's not that I don't like her story. I do. It's just that I've heard it so many times I find myself doubting there could possibly be anything fresh left to say about it. But in all my years of hearing about the Samaritan woman, reading her story, and feeling like I know it, I missed something. Something really big.

Right smack dab in the middle of one of the longest recorded interactions Jesus has with a woman, He starts talking about food.

Food! And I'd never picked up on it before. I somehow missed Jesus' crucial teaching that our bodies must have two kinds of nourishment: physical and spiritual.

Just as I must have physical food for my body to survive, I have to have spiritual food for my soul to thrive. Jesus says, "My food ... is to do the will of him who sent me and to finish his work" (John 4:34). And then He goes on to say, "I tell you, open your eyes and look at the fields! They are ripe for harvest" (John 4:35b).

There is a bigger plan here! Don't get distracted by physical food. Don't think physical food can satisfy the longing of your soul. Only Jesus can do this. Our souls were created to crave Him and love others to Him. So many people are waiting to hear the message of your calling. Don't get stuck in defeat and held back from it.

In the midst of offering salvation to the Samaritan woman, Jesus seems to wander off on this tangent about food. But it's not a tangent at all. Actually, it fits perfectly. It relates directly to the core issue of spiritual malnutrition. Specifically, it's about trying to use food to fill not only the physical void of our stomachs but also the spiritual void of our souls. For years, I've been physically overweight but spiritually underweight. How crucial it is for us to remember:

> *Food can fill our stomachs but never our souls.*
> *Possessions can fill our houses but never our hearts.*
> *Sex can fill our nights but never our hunger for love.*
> *Children can fill our days but never our identities.*

Jesus wants us to know only He can fill us and truly satisfy us. He really wants us to really believe that.

Only by being filled with authentic soul food from Jesus—following Him and telling others about Him—will our souls ever be truly satisfied. And breaking free from consuming thoughts about food allows us to see and pursue our calling with more confidence and clarity.

*Dear Lord, I know that it is true that only You can fill me.
I acknowledge that You are the Lord of my life. I want
to please You today in all that I do. Help me to follow You.
In Jesus' name. Amen.*

DAY 57

Well Pleased

And a voice from heaven said,
"This is my Son, whom I love;
with him I am well pleased."
(MATTHEW 3:17)

Thought for the Day: Daily, hourly, and moment by moment, I must stand in the reality of my God-given identity.

When I was a young child, before my dad abandoned our family, I dressed in my best dress and twirled before him. I was desperate to hear words of love and affirmation he never gave me. In my teen years, I tried to earn his attention by performing well and getting good grades. But no matter how well I performed, my dad didn't stay. He didn't love me. He didn't approve of me.

This kind of hurt sinks deep into the longing heart of a girl.

It's probably no surprise that I used the same approach with my heavenly Father. I thought I had to perform for His approval. For years, I did the religious dance of Bible study, ministry leadership, prayer, and service to gain God's approval. Instead of doing these things because I was loved, I did them *so that* I'd be loved. It's important to be mindful of this dynamic so we don't link our food struggles to a similar kind of performance mentality.

Have you ever struggled with feeling like a "good Christian" when you exercised self-control and feeling like a "bad Christian" when you didn't? We must chat about this. While we do want to gain spiritual perspectives while losing the weight, we must resist slipping into performance mode.

In the Gospels, God makes a powerful statement about Jesus: "This is my Son, whom I love; with him I am well pleased" (Matthew 3:17).

I found new perspective in this passage when I realized that Jesus had not yet gone to the cross, performed miracles, or led the masses. His Father affirmed Jesus' identity *before* Jesus started His public ministry. Jesus heard God, believed God, and remained filled.

In Christ, God has given us a new identity (Romans 6:4). But, unlike Christ, we tend to forget who we are and to fill our lives with endless activities to prove our worth and significance. We do this to earn love and approval from other people as well as from God. Our humanity makes us hungry people. It is similar to the phenomenon of being satisfied with a large dinner one evening only to wake up the next morning feeling famished. Truth comes in and fills us up, but we can't expect one serving of truth to feed us for a lifetime. Our emotional cracks, crevices, and life circumstances are like drain holes that leak the truth and leave behind only hollowness.

Therefore, we must stand moment by moment in the truth of our identity before we resume our daily activities and even our healthy eating efforts. Grasp the truth and rub it in deep. Let it fill the drain holes that leach away your significance. Hear God say,

"You are my daughter, whom I love; with you I am well pleased." Well pleased because of who you are, not what you do. Well pleased because of an unfathomable, unconditional love — a love not earned but simply given.

And isn't it interesting that right after we read God's affirmation of Jesus in Matthew 3, the very next chapter starts off with Jesus being tempted with food while fasting in the desert? But because Jesus was filled with truth, He didn't engage the enemy. Remember? He deflected Satan's lies by repeatedly quoting Scripture. He remained steady, believing who He was and whose He was. His identity was established before His ministry activities began.

When we know our identity *before* we jump into activity, we don't have to guess how to handle the vicious lies of the enemy. We don't need to displace God with inappropriate physical pleasure or material comforts. We don't need to crave the acceptance of others. Because in God we are loved, accepted, and whole.

Oh, may this statement straight from God be inscribed, engraved, and tattooed in the most permanent of ways on our hearts: "Well pleased ... well pleased ... well pleased."

God loves you, sweet sister. Rest in this reality today.

Dear Lord, I don't often feel that You are well pleased with me. Help me to change my perspective and remember that You love me regardless of what I do. You loved me before I was even born. And You are well pleased with me now. Help me to live like I believe this today. In Jesus' name. Amen.

DAY 58

Condemnation vs. Conviction

But thanks be to God that, though you used to be slaves to sin,
you have come to obey from your heart the pattern of teaching
that has now claimed your allegiance. You have been set free
from sin and have become slaves to righteousness.

(ROMANS 6:17–18)

Thought for the Day: Condemnation defeats us.
Conviction unlocks the greatest potential for change.

When an airline recently lost my friend Holly's luggage, I was elected to go to the lost luggage office and see what could be done. The woman behind the counter saw me coming and held her hand up with a quick and cutting, "Don't even come in here until you've looked through the pile to the left."

So much for flying the friendly skies. I dutifully looked through the pile of homeless luggage and there wasn't one suitcase that looked anything like Holly's. So I proceeded to walk toward the office again.

"You didn't look!" yelled the woman behind the counter. "I told you to look *through* that pile."

I swallowed. Hard.

"I did look and I can guarantee you the piece of luggage I'm looking for isn't there," I said.

She rolled her eyes, motioned for me to approach her desk, and continued to do everything in her power to act as if losing Holly's suitcase was somehow my fault. I dealt with it. And dealt with it. And then got tired of dealing with it.

"Look," I snapped, "I am the customer here. Your airline lost our luggage. I wish I didn't have to be in this little office right now. But I am because it is your job to help me. And that's exactly what I need you to do ... your job."

I didn't raise my voice. But I did raise my intensity. I let the situation dictate my reaction, and I walked away feeling frustrated but justified. Until an hour later. I had this nagging sense I'd blown it. I started thinking of several of my gentle friends who never would have talked sharply or gotten caught up in their frustration: *Amy wouldn't have acted that way. Samantha would have used this as a golden opportunity to love the unlovely. Ann would have given so much grace, a revival would have taken place right there in the lost luggage office and years later this lady would be sharing her testimony of how everything changed the day that kind woman came to her office.*

Ugh. Shame slithered up close and whispered, "Look at you and all your Bible studying ... what good is it all? What good are you?" The heaviness in my soul left me with this sinking feeling that I would never really be able to change. And a familiar thought ran through a well-worn pattern in my brain: *I'll probably always be a slave to the raw emotions that catch me off guard.*

What a lie.

If you're believing this same lie, hang on to this truth: Just the fact that you're reading this book is a sign of great progress. Refuse to wallow in the depressing angst condemnation brings. On the other hand, embrace any conviction you feel. Condemnation defeats us. Conviction unlocks the greatest potential for change.

Conviction is a call to action, like the warning light on the dashboard of a car. What call to action can you embrace today to make even more imperfect progress? As for me, I'm deciding in advance to have compassion on people like the woman at the luggage counter. Obviously, something hard in her life caused her to display the attitude she did. When I imagine her hurt, I soften my reaction. Indeed, conviction leads to the greatest potential for me to change.

Dear Lord, show me where I have believed the lies that condemnation speaks. You've set me free, and I long to live in that truth. In Jesus' name. Amen.

DAY 59

God, I'm a Little Mad and a Lot Confused

Trust in the LORD with all your heart
and lean not on your own understanding;
in all your ways submit to him,
and he will make your paths straight.

(PROVERBS 3:5 – 6)

Thought for the Day:
God is big enough to handle our honest feelings.

Kick off your shoes and get ready to get gut-honest. When God doesn't seem to be answering our prayers, it can be hard. Sometimes, downright awful.

One minute, I'm determined to trust God. The next, I feel myself questioning God. The "why" questions tumble in so hard. My heart hurts. My tears fall. And in those raw moments I just feel a little mad and a lot confused.

Ever been there?

I don't want to oversimplify what to do in these times. Facing issues that never seem to stop is tough. Really tough. Especially those situations where the answers aren't easy or clean-cut. But I have discovered three things that help me when God seems silent.

1. Press into God when you want to pull away.

When I really want to hear from God, but He seems silent, I sometimes find I want to disengage from my normal spiritual activities. Skip church. Put my Bible on the shelf. And let more and more time lapse between prayers.

But pulling away only makes things worse. God says, "You will seek me and find me when you seek me with all your heart" (Jeremiah 29:13). All my heart includes the parts that are broken. Bring it all to God.

He can handle your honesty and will respond. But we have to go where truth is. Go to church. Listen to praise music. Read the Bible. Memorize verses. And keep talking to God.

2. Praise God out loud when you want to get lost in complaints.

In the midst of whatever you're facing, find simple things for which to praise God. I don't mean thank Him for the hard stuff. I mean thank Him for the other simple, good things you still experience. A child's laugh. A bush that blooms. The warmth of a blanket. The gift of this breath and then the next.

Scripture reminds me that praise leads to newness: "He put a new song in my mouth, a song of praise to our God; many will see and fear and will trust in the LORD" (Psalm 40:3 NASB). We can literally find new words with which to process life in a more positive way when we choose to praise God instead of complain.

3. Put yourself in the company of truth.

That friend who speaks truth? Listen to her. Stay connected to her. Let her speak truth into your life even when you're tired of hearing it. As Proverbs 12:26 (NASB) encourages, "The righteous is a guide to his neighbor." Stand in the shadow of her faith when you feel your own faith is weak. Let her lead you back to God time and time again.

It's okay to feel a little mad and a lot confused. Our God is big enough to handle our honest feelings. But don't let your feelings lead you away from God or away from His truth. Press into Him. Praise Him. And put yourself in the company of truth. As you stay with God in these ways, you will be ready to receive His answer when it comes.

Dear Lord, thank You for understanding me, even when I'm mad or confused. I pray I would daily be intentional in coming close to You and praising You. Help me to find a good friend whom I can trust to speak truth into my life. In Jesus' name. Amen.

DAY 60

Ruined for Good

Fools show their annoyance at once,
but the prudent overlook an insult.
(PROVERBS 12:16)

Thought for the Day: I have to make the choice every day to interrupt my fleshly tendencies of yelling and getting angry over minor things.

If you have kids, then I'm sure you've felt the frustration of having things ruined. Maybe you've experienced grape juice on the carpet, scratches on hardwood floors, permanent ink on your favorite shirt, or something similar.

My daughter, Ashley, once went up the stairway with a crayon putting tick marks on our freshly painted walls with each step she took. Then she dragged the crayon all the way down the hall to her room. Yes, I said freshly painted walls. I wanted to pull my hair out by the roots!

I'd like to be a mom who handles mishaps and messes with a graceful, "That's okay, dear." But I'm wired with firecrackers in my blood. So I have to make the choice to let the Holy Spirit rein me in. This means getting into God's Word every day and praying for Him to help me display grace, patience, and self-control when I want to do the exact opposite.

I have to make the choice every day to invite God's Spirit to interrupt my fleshly tendencies of yelling and getting so angry over minor things. As Proverbs 12:16 says, I don't want to be a fool that shows my annoyance at once. I want to be a prudent, wise woman. I want to be a woman who doesn't constantly regret my reactions later.

God helps me with this through perspective changers. He shows me a different way to look at and process things that trigger my emotions. In response to my frustration with my kids ruining things, He gave me a sweet change of perspective that improved my outlook and diffused my anger.

While visiting my husband's parents, I took a liking to a writing desk in their home. I mentioned to Art's mom that I'd love to have it if she ever decided to get rid of it. But she was quick to tell me that she would never get rid of it because it was priceless.

She unlatched the fold-down lid to reveal what made this desk so special to her. In a little boy's handwriting, the letters A-R-T were scratched onto the surface. His name was forever carved onto her desk.

She admitted to being angry with Art when this happened years and years ago, but now the scratches that seemed to have ruined her desk are priceless treasures to her. Her little boy's handwriting is saved for her to cherish and remember. The desk had been ruined ... for good.

And I pray that remembering this story, this perspective change, makes me ruined for good as well.

Dear Lord, thank You for perspective changes that help us to see past the here and now so that we can see Your truth which sets us free. We are freed from anger, firecracker emotions, short fuses, and explosive tempers ... free to reveal the You in us! In Jesus' name. Amen.

About Lysa TerKeurst

Lysa TerKeurst is a wife to Art and mom to five priority blessings named Jackson, Mark, Hope, Ashley, and Brooke. The author of more than a dozen books, including the *New York Times*-bestselling *Made to Crave*, she has been featured on *Focus on the Family*, *Good Morning America*, the *Oprah Winfrey Show*, and in *O Magazine*. Her greatest passion is inspiring women to say yes to God and take part in the awesome adventure He has designed every soul to live. While she is the cofounder of Proverbs 31 Ministries, to those who know her best she is simply a car-pooling mom who loves her family, loves Jesus passionately, and struggles like the rest of us with laundry, junk drawers, and cellulite.

WEBSITE: If you enjoyed this book by Lysa, you'll love all the additional resources found at *www.Ungluedbook.com*, *www.MadeToCrave.org*, *www.LysaTerKeurst.com*, and *www.Proverbs31.org*.

BLOG: Dialog with Lysa through her daily blog, see pictures of her family, and follow her speaking schedule. She'd love to meet you at an event in your area! *www.LysaTerKeurst.com*.

A Gift Just for You

Get these free colorful key tags to keep you inspired and on track.
Place your order by emailing: resources@Proverbs31.org and reference
"Unglued Key Tags" in the subject line. The only charge is $1 to cover
shipping and handling. Bulk orders for Bible studies and small groups
are also available with special shipping rates.

About Proverbs 31 Ministries

If you were inspired by the *Unglued Devotional* and desire to deepen
your own personal relationship with Jesus Christ, I encourage you to
connect with Proverbs 31 Ministries. Proverbs 31 Ministries exists to be
a trusted friend who will take you by the hand and walk by your side,
leading you one step closer to the heart of God, through:

· *Encouragement for Today,*
Free Online Daily Devotions

· The *P31 Woman* Monthly Magazine

· Daily Radio Programs

For more information about Proverbs 31 Ministries, visit:
www.Proverbs31.org

To inquire about having Lysa speak at your event, email:
info@lysaterkeurst.com

Unglued

Making Wise Choices in the Midst of Raw Emotions

Lysa TerKeurst,
New York Times *Bestselling Author*

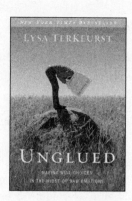

God gave us emotions to experience life, not destroy it! Lysa TerKeurst admits that she, like most women, has had experiences where others bump into her happy and she comes emotionally unglued. We stuff, we explode, or we react somewhere in between. What do we do with these raw emotions? Is it really possible to make emotions work for us instead of against us? Yes, and in her usual inspiring and practical way, Lysa will show you how. Filled with gut-honest personal examples and biblical teaching, *Unglued* will equip you to:

- Know with confidence how to resolve conflict in your important relationships.

- Find peace in your most difficult relationships as you learn to be honest but kind when offended.

- Identify what type of reactor you are and how to significantly improve your communication.

- Respond with no regrets by managing your tendencies to stuff or explode.

- Gain a deep sense of calm by responding to situations out of your control.

Available in stores and online!

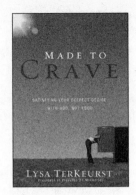